Open Your Eyes
Toward Living More Deeply in the Present

Blessings & peace —

Gail Stearns

11/10

Open Your Eyes
Toward Living More Deeply in the Present

GAIL J. STEARNS

WIPF & STOCK · Eugene, Oregon

OPEN YOUR EYES TOWARD LIVING MORE DEEPLY IN THE PRESENT

Wipf & Stock
An Imprint of Wipf and Stock Publishers
199 W. 8th Ave., Suite 3
Eugene, OR 97401
www.wipfandstock.com

ISBN 13: 978-1-60899-635-3

Manufactured in the U.S.A.

For my parents

Contents

Acknowledgments

I WOULD like to thank my friends and readers Sharon Kehoe and Michael Jorn for their comments and challenges on the first draft of this book. I am grateful to Nancy Nydegger for her careful editing on a later draft. I thank my sister, Nancy Martin, not only for her editing expertise, but for being my friend and confidant throughout the process of writing and living through all the events I describe in this book. And my thanks to Christian Amondson and the editors at Wipf & Stock for their willingness to take on this project.

I was allowed the gift of time to spend with my family, as well as to travel, read, and begin this book during a sabbatical granted by The Common Ministry Council, and received support for that time through a Sabbatical Grant for Pastoral Leaders from the Louisville Institute. Thank you both.

I am deeply grateful to all the persons named and referred to in this book. Although I use only first names or references, you know who you are, and you are integral to this story. I especially want to thank my close friends, Carolea Webb, Carol Hoeksema, Kristine Zakarison, Libby Walker, Terry Keller, and Sharon Kehoe. Like the women in Mark, they know what it means to be present for a friend, and I'm grateful for our time together discussing theology, practicing vocation, and sharing meditations.

My professors and colleagues of many years have helped me to interweave theology and practice, which I endeavor to do with this book. The many students I have taught and ministered to throughout the years have taught me more than they can know. Members of the Interfaith Dialog have educated me a great deal about their respective religious traditions, about the process of the

Acknowledgments

interfaith journey, and about what it means to truly listen to one another.

Finally, I thank my family, especially my kids, John and Jeana, for all they teach me and for enriching my life. Thanks too to my sister, Jane Upmeyer, and to my parents, Ben and Mary Stearns, who have always encouraged me both to believe and to question.

Introduction

Searching for Peace

I GREW up in the church. I was taught that if we were decent people and lived right most of the time, we would be rewarded. I learned that if I was troubled or feeling distant from God, the answer could be found in praying more, or perhaps through finding a new worship service or joining a Bible study. But it was never enough.

As I have sought a way of inner peace and a means for reconciliation for our world, meditation teachers from Christianity, Judaism, Sufism and Buddhism have taught me how to sit in Presence (what some call God) or to be fully in the present moment. I have learned from Native and Goddess traditions about valuing the earth, not just seeking other-worldly glory. I have witnessed in the lives of Muslim friends, as well as in communities of Benedictine sisters and ecumenical Christian brothers what it means to live a life of daily ritual, prayer, and silence. Jewish and Christian scholars have led me toward a new way to read scripture and understand Jesus.

In the end, I feel a little like Dorothy in the Wizard of Oz. What I have come to understand is that all the discoveries I unearthed in other religions and spiritual traditions are also available in Christianity.

Within our lives lies peace. It is as close as our heart, and as easy to reach as touching the person next to us. It is peace found not in our past or our future, not in the government or our relationships or even our religion—it is peace that is found now. In this very moment. This is the peace of living in the present in a radical way we witness in the life of Jesus.

Our search for spiritual fulfillment and for global reconciliation today is taking many people beyond Christianity to discover varieties of other spiritual paths. This is leaving many Christians worried about heresy, while at the same time strangely unfulfilled within. But spiritual fulfillment is *also* possible through Christianity, as we open ourselves to a new way to understand Jesus. Because Jesus has been understood so narrowly, many today dismiss Christianity as no longer useful. Yet the way of Jesus uniquely presents a centuries-old truth of radical peace and presence for individuals and for the world.

The argument of this book may feel backwards—it is not an apology for Christianity, nor is it a claim there is only one way to salvation, inner peace or peace in our world. Rather, it offers a new way to recover ancient truth that can still be viable and life-giving for us today, in an era during which we are witnessing an unprecedented explosion in varieties of spiritual quests, coupled with the urgent need for global peace.

As searching people we long for grounding in our own lives, for a way to understand the Divine or God or Jesus or Something Greater than ourselves in a real, palpable way—because, while we know that Presence is there, we don't quite feel it. Some of us tell ourselves that everything is all right because it's in God's hands, and others say everything's ok due to some kind of karma, although we don't really understand how those concepts work or even if we really believe them. We long to know that everything really is going to be all right, and that it is actually as it should be right now. Jesus addresses in his followers this longing to understand and be fully present when he uses words such as listen, sit, and watch.

People of all religions and spiritual paths long for a better world. Jesus calls it the "reign (kingdom) of God"—a world described in other ways in other religions—where compassion and justice reign, where children do not go hungry at night, where wars are not waged by invoking religious principles that defy the very religions they purport to champion.

In order, however, to see what Jesus really meant by these words and phrases, whether we identify ourselves within or outside of Christianity, we have to suspend much of what we have been taught and have held to be sacrosanct within Christianity. We have to open our eyes, to borrow a metaphor Jesus often used.

My friend Edward is a pastor in Cameroon. In a culture that emerges from Tribal Religion and now has a large percentage of Muslims, he talks to me about meeting the Christians and the joy in their worship together, as he moves about the country. It is almost like receiving a letter from the apostle Paul when I hear him talk. I do not doubt the connection Christians share across the geography of his land. I do not live in the world of "the Christians," however. Where I live, the belief systems are so varied that I never know what I will encounter. This is especially true on a university campus, where intellectual discussion constantly deconstructs doctrine and faith. It is also true because the church has become so tied to its dogma and rules and limited in its understanding of God that many find themselves outside that definition and are either blatantly anti-religious or are seeking truth through other spiritual paths. In my capacity as director of an ecumenical campus ministry dedicated to interfaith work, set within a university where I also teach, I simply cannot make assumptions when students, faculty or staff members walk through my office door. I do not presume what beliefs they hold or the depth of pain they carry despite outer confidence, or their religious affiliation, or primary sexual or racial identity. Rather, I should say that when I do jump to conclusions and make assumptions, I am often wrong.

Many of us are questioning. This book is for the dozens of students who sit in my office, or more often stand with a cup of coffee in the kitchen of our campus ministry building, and dare to voice their doubts with me. I cannot tell you how many times I have heard the phrase, "I'm not sure I believe in God anymore."

And each time a student and I probe further and I suggest this question may be a sign the student is taking his or her faith seriously, and even deepening in faith, he or she is always surprised. "I was told it meant I was losing my faith," is the inevitable response. Told by a well-meaning friend, by a leader in a campus Christian organization, by a relative. My heart breaks when I think of all the college students who have not found a faculty or pastor's office or a campus ministry kitchen or a nonjudgmental ear somewhere— anywhere—to tell them radical faith exploration is worthwhile.

Many are afraid to entertain questions. Often, those of us who would claim to have the deepest faith in Christ seem to trust him the least. I recall a woman who approached me after I finished a presentation for parents of incoming freshman, about religious groups on campus. She was anxious that her son continue in college with the same para-church organization he had participated in throughout high school, and was deeply fearful that he might fall backward in his faith if he didn't. I responded that he may or may not find that group a good fit at college, but suggested she could trust God with her son's faith exploration and future life of faith. She looked at me quite startled, as if that had not occurred to her before.

This book is for numerous people in our society who may or may not attend church regularly, but call themselves Christians, volunteer in food banks, participate in book studies, or teach Sunday School, yet still feel un fulfilled. I think of a woman who recently went through a new member class then was denied the opportunity to join the church, when in her statement of faith she admitted she was not sure Jesus was the only way to salvation. I think of my friend Michael, who was raised a Christian, later pursued his own intellectual and spiritual journey apart from the church, and at mid-life finds himself drawn to a church community, but still asking, "Why be a Christian?" I think of thousands of people who sit patiently Sunday after Sunday without voicing their doubts that there is just this one way to understand Jesus, or their certainty that God will not condemn those that do not properly confess their faith.

There are those who do speak their voice, but are in the minority. I have found such mentors in surprising places in my life. Especially when I have struggled with decisions in my ministry, I have found counsel with elders who have struggled with issues of vocation, personalities, politics, and faith. Al, who was approaching 90 years at the time, was a source of wisdom when I felt unsure how to proceed at work. He told me stories from his professional life and encouraged me to let go of having to have all the answers. Leonard, an elder in the church I first pastored, and later Dick, in his 80s, took time to discuss my sermons when I knew others found them a bit on the edge—and pushed me to challenge rigid, moralistic understandings of Christianity even further. Having respectively lived through the premature death of a son, learned to deal with headstrong fundamentalist Christian relatives, and come to fully accept a daughter's lesbianism, and each having the courage to let go and change on a road of compassion, taught them deep wisdom. This book is in gratitude for guidance by these elders and other women and men like them.

I write for countless people, like myself, who yearn to live in a way that brings meaning to our lives. Many of us live with pain, whether it is emotional pain caused by broken relationships or life hardship, or physical pain due to disease. We long to make sense of it. People who suffer have been told it is somehow necessary to teach them true faith (usually a lesson told by those who suffer less than they do), or that suffering is something they can eradicate if they just believe. Suffering is part of life, and one of our most powerful teachers and companions in this world. I know for me, it was not until I experienced uninvited suffering myself, and through that began to see that people daily live suffering, dying, and renewing lives, that I fully began to understand how we can live with the reality of suffering. Suffering was part of the life of Jesus and it is part of ours. Jesus teaches us a way to understand human suffering in our personal lives and live more deeply in the present.

We live in a world that is groaning under the weight of over-population, environmental destruction, devastation from natural disasters, incomprehensible human cruelty in ethnic warring, poverty and struggle. Corporately, we yearn for understanding and an end to this immense suffering. Learning to live with the realities of pain and brokenness, and coming to appreciate Jesus in a new way moves us toward compassion for all who suffer. This journey will move us to work to bring about the realm of God on earth, a realm in which we will inflict less suffering and live in greater peace.

A major stumbling block for many of us centers upon our rigid definitions of who the real followers of Jesus are. When our rules and regulations separate us as humans we cannot see this new way of compassion calling us to be one human family. Consider the exclusive, yet arbitrary laws determining who is eligible to become a leader in the church and represent the Holy as a priest, pastor or church lay leader. Denominations draw lines that do nothing more than cause greater rifts and create pain as they declare some to be "right" enough to be ordained as a pastoral or lay leader. That rightness is usually due to some fact of birth, such as being born male, a requirement in some churches still today; or heterosexual, required by many—traits science tells us a person has no control over in the first place. These regulations can serve to encourage those of us who are born "right" to feel more and more righteous, rather than teach us a way of humility that leads to reconciliation.

My friend Greg is a person with enormous gifts to share and a heart equally as large. He and I sit together in church on occasion. He shares with me how saddened he is that the church asks him to sing in the choir, sit in the pew, listen to sermons on Sundays, and give his money, yet it outright tells him he is not even eligible to be considered for service on the governing board of the church as a gay man.

Jesus came to bring the reign of God to earth—a new way if we follow him. Not a jealous, competitive, one-upmanship way; not a contest; not a Truth that condemns all others. Rather, Jesus came to bring a way of reconciliation and love. He demonstrated living peacefully and confidently in the present. He showed us a reign on earth that moves us together toward peace, a world where we all sit down at the table together, where diseases are healed and hunger is curbed. A way that welcomes peace, and moves toward an end to poverty and war.

It is time to call a truce to claiming the superiority of our religion over others. It is time to stop insisting upon the Truth of our religion that trumps others. It is time to stop claiming that we are saved and they are not. That we are right and they are wrong. It is really time to stop litmus tests of who is called Christian. If we want to fully understand what Jesus taught and what it means to be a Christian, we have to step outside our comfort zones and suspend our suspicions of everyone else. We have to set aside our fears and stop being afraid of anyone different than us.

Many persons understand that sources of wisdom are unexpected. People like Paul, a gifted musician, who drew from the wisdom of many religious traditions to compose music for *Mosaic,* a contemplative worship experience a team of my colleagues and students developed featuring music, readings and silence. Many, like Paul, understand revelation emerges from many sources and various religions.

Christopher, a young man who attended *Mosaic* regularly our first year, and seemed to find deep meaning in the worship, approached me after worship with a question. He said on that particular evening he was having trouble finding the Christian connection with a song based upon words from the *Tao Te Ching,* that included a series of paradoxical statements: "Yield and overcome. Bend and be straight. Empty and be full. Wear out and be new."[1] Although it was not always necessary for me to find the Christian

1. "Tao Te Ching #22" from Smith, *Mosaic.*

connection, I responded that I hear in this song the paradox of faith. Jesus evokes this when he says that if we lose ourselves, we will be saved. Some may call this not a paradox, but rather a continuum of faith and reality. Letting go and finding the opposite of what we previously held to be most important is central in the teachings and parables of Jesus.

In this way, we come to understand that the *Tao Te Ching* includes themes that are deeply Christian, and Jesus' message holds wisdom central to the Tao. Others have made such connections between the life of Jesus and the deepest message of their religious teacher. Thich Nhat Hanh's *Living Buddha, Living Christ* uncovers similarities in the teachings of the Buddha and Christ.

We have much to learn from our brothers and sisters in various religious traditions. We can glean wisdom from traditions that stress the way of living (orthopraxy), like Taoism, and seek the spiritual foundations of those that focus more on doctrine (orthodoxy), like Islam. We can learn from the centrality of one of the five pillars of Islam, for example, that of engaging in charity. Although, like Christianity, throughout history Muslims have not always lived up the ideal, many have, and the discipline of caring has been central to Islamic spirituality for hundreds of years.[2] Muhammad writes, "Feed the hungry and visit the sick, and free the captives . . . Assist any person oppressed, whether Muslim or non-Muslim."[3]

This is not to say that all religions are the same. The diversity of religion is a gift in this world, with its various rituals, traditions, practices and wisdom, differences we would not want to erase. Our task is not to prove religions are all the same, or that we all seek the same God. Nor is it just to claim that Jesus was simply a Buddhist, or a mystic. But we have much to learn from those religions that more fully integrate charity and mysticism than does Christianity.

2. Armstrong, *Islam*, 186.
3. Al-Suhrawardy, *Wisdom of Muhammad*, 99.

We also seek to honor Jesus as the Christ. The beauty and uniqueness of Christianity lies in the reality that the Divine, the way to know the Divine in Presence here, now and eternally, and the way to usher in heaven on earth is all revealed to us incarnationally, in the person of Jesus Christ.

If we began by focusing on that unique incarnation and the wisdom we saw in Jesus, we would eat with tax collectors and lepers, instead of those who sing the same songs and profess the same beliefs we do. If we paid attention to the wisdom we learn from Jesus and many religions, we would start with compassion instead of doctrine. If we believed we were here to help usher in a world reflecting real peace rather than human politics, Christianity would become a whole different religion—probably not even recognizable.

Startlingly, Christianity might even look pretty similar and bring about the same kind of world that other religions would help bring about if people took the teachings of Abraham, Mohammad, Lao Tzu or the Buddha deeply to heart. Selflessness, compassion, letting go of our own grasping egos and opening our hearts to others, charity—these are core in all world religions that have stood the tests of time.

Persons learn through many spiritual paths to live in the presence of what some call God, to be deeply centered, and to discover peace out of pain. People learn compassion for others through a variety of spiritual, human and religious journeys. It has been argued that today we need a spiritual transformation equal to current explosions of technology and communication.[4] Some claim there is a new spirituality and a transformation in human consciousness that is desperately needed, and even now beginning to occur outside of religion.[5] What we have been missing is that these truths are *also* to be found within Christianity when we stop seeing the religion as a way that is superior and right, but rather

4. Helminski, *Living Presence*, x.
5. Tolle, *A New Earth*, 17–18.

as revelation that comes in a unique way through the gift of a real person, who we know as Jesus the Christ.

In this book, I begin with a reading of Jesus and discussion of our understanding of God in order to open our eyes to a new way to live a more compassionate life. Chapters One and Two form the framework to understand Jesus in a more progressive way, and to broaden our concept of God toward living continually in God's presence and the mystery of life. Chapters Three and Four describe ways to live in this Presence through meditation, awareness, coming to know ourselves more deeply, and letting go of our egos. Chapters Five and Six tackle the problem of suffering. Chapter Five includes a brief account of my own story, not because it is unique to me in its intensity in any way, but because it is where my understanding of living with suffering blossomed. Chapter Six focuses on the meaning of the cross and suffering in Jesus' life, as well as in the lives of several contemporary people of faith. Chapter Seven turns to our life in community. Given what we have learned about the meaning of Jesus' life, how can we live in community in a way to continue the compassionate ministry he began? Recent theologies and current examples of ministry help guide our quest toward living in a world more open to our awareness of God and the present.

A NOTE ON POINT OF VIEW
AND BIBLICAL INTERPRETATION

In order to glean the central meaning in Jesus' ministry, I focus on the gospel of Mark, the shortest and earliest of the four gospels, closest to the actual life and Galilean context of Jesus himself. It is believed to have been written near the destruction of the Temple in Jerusalem in 70C.E.[6] The later three gospels each have a different

---

6. One passage that helps scholars to date the gospel of Mark near 70 C.E. is found in Mark 13, where Jesus is quoted as giving an apocalyptic speech about a time when his followers would be tested. Some scholars see it as authentic words of Jesus placed here by Mark for the benefit of his current

focus in their telling of Jesus' life as they were composed by different authors for different audiences.[7]

I utilize many strategies in my reading of the gospel of Mark, including seeking to understand what the author we call Mark wanted his readers to understand, or the way readers today engage with the text in search of meaning (sometimes called reader-response criticism). I read Mark as a whole story or piece of literature, including forms and metaphor (literary or narrative criticism), and at times surmise what Mark interprets from earlier stories he received about Jesus (redaction criticism). I consider the historical and social context of the times (historical criticism). I bring to Mark a feminist reading, considering within the text and context relations of power in biblical society, in the writing of the gospel, and in interpretation of the gospel today. These relations of power include, but are not limited to, gender relations. All these forms of criticism I have learned from teachers and scholars of the New Testament.[8]

I see Mark's gospel not as a fully developed Christology, or theology of Jesus as the Messiah, as that theology was still in

readers who were being led astray by false prophets, and facing the impending fall of the Temple in Jerusalem. This event took place in 70 C.E. See Collins, *Mark*, 14. Others hold that Mark wrote immediately after the destruction of the Temple. See Crossan and Reed, *Excavating Jesus*, 225, and further discussion in Crossan, *The Historical Jesus*, 356–9.

7. Mark has been found to be used as a source for the authors of the Gospels of Matthew and Luke, who also shared a second source, labeled "Q," that has been lost to us. John tells the gospel story independently in form and emphasis.

8. See the Introduction to Anderson & Moore, *Mark & Method*, for an excellent and understandable review of the types of criticism that have been used for reading Mark. Each successive chapter is an application of a different type of biblical criticism. Collins also demonstrates various methods in her meticulously detailed commentary on Mark. See also Rhoads, et al. for a detailed exposition of Mark through the lens of narrative criticism. Borg, in *Conversations with Scripture*, unpacks Mark largely through a historical-metaphorical approach. Finally, St. Clair writes from a Womanist perspective and analyzes Mark using a sociolinguistic model in *Call and Consequences*.

formation when Mark was written. I like Adela Yarbro Collins' description of the gospel of Mark as "interpretation" of the life of Jesus.[9]

Having said all that, I do not write as a biblical scholar. I hold a doctorate in gender theory, and study and teach issues of gender and of religion. I am of Nordic and Irish descent, middle-class, raised in the Midwest, a mother, an ordained minister of the Presbyterian Church (U.S.A.), and director of an ecumenical campus ministry with interfaith commitments, situated at a secular university in the Western U.S.

I write mainly as a pastor. You might think of this as material that forms the background of a sermon, or informs acts of pastoral care. This is a practical book for progressive people of faith. My interest is to remove Mark's grip from literal readings that attempt to dictate how we should live and open the way for new understandings of how we do live, here and now, faithfully and fully. I read Mark as interpretive story and in doing so aim to help us understand in even deeper ways the complexities of suffering, joy and meaning in our lives.

9. Collins, *Mark*, 44. Collins also uses the term "portrayal," and Rhoads, et. al., describe the gospel story as Mark's "portrayal" of Jesus in *Mark as Story*, 5.

1

Understanding Jesus

JESUS IS not the only way. Jesus is more than that. Jesus shows us not for the first or last time what it means to live a deep, spiritual life, but in a unique way as we witness a human being on earth living fully in the present, and in the presence of what many name God. In the person Jesus we observe a way of presence and prayer—a way to remain centered whether in the midst of suffering or joy. And we can understand that presence in our own lives to include the living Christ. This can help us let go of our own fabricated, frantic worlds, and find a rich and grounded life.

Consider the story told in the gospel of Mark about Jesus healing the woman who has been bleeding for twelve years. Jesus is standing with a huge crowd "thronged about him." Then suddenly he asks, "Who touched my garments?"[1] How can a person that is surrounded by all this noise, bumping and chaos, know someone touched the hem of his garment? Even the disciples are incredulous and ask how in the world Jesus knows she touched him, with the crowds pressing around him.

In a situation like that, most of us would be thinking about the future, especially how to get closer to Jesus ourselves, or how to get out of the crowd unscathed, or questioning why we got our-

---

1. Mark 5:24–34. Biblical references are taken from *The New Oxford Annotated Bible, Revised Standard Version*, unless otherwise noted. At times I take liberty with gender terms, such as changing "Man" to "Humanity" or "he" to "she" to reflect a translation of "anthropos" as human, rather than man, and to acknowledge the presence of women as well as men among Jesus' followers.

selves into the crowd in the first place. We would likely be annoyed at the bumping, and the noise would be giving us a headache. We might regret that we didn't eat earlier, because we would assume we definitely wouldn't find any food in this crowd. We certainly would not be attuned to the touch of a bleeding woman on the hem of our garment in the midst of the present chaos. How does Jesus know? He perceives that power has gone out from him. Jesus is completely aware of what is happening in the present moment.

LIVING IN THE PRESENT

How often do we miss what is going on right here and now? How often are we really present? Think of the things that are occurring within and around you right now—are you aware that you are breathing as you read this book? Do you know how your body feels—that maybe your left leg is sore or your right arm is stiff? Do you realize there are sounds around you—perhaps dogs barking, or birds singing, or car engines, or planes flying overhead, or music playing, or people talking? One of the ways we can become aware of the present is to listen—to quiet our thoughts and feelings about the past and future, and just listen.

Ancient wisdom teaches us that being grounded comes through awareness of the absolute present. Too often we live in the past—not really awake right now. We have said something that may have been offensive to another, or even truly hurt someone, and we spend our time obsessing over feelings of guilt. We reminisce, remember, regret, recall—all of which take us into the past. Sometimes the feelings that are stirred by those thoughts are so strong we are even unable to function. We may feel so much guilt, perhaps having done something that will change our life or someone else's forever, that our present is colored completely by that past action. We may have panic attacks, fail to get out of bed and do our work, or distance ourselves from others because we feel ashamed.

Alternatively, we may feel we were wronged by another's past actions. In our anger, we fume, fantasize about what we will say or do in return, and fabricate dozens of scenarios about what would have happened if this had not been done to us. Dwelling in our guilt or our anger over something that occurred in the past, we are not living in the present at all. We are living with the thoughts and feelings created as we focus on the past.

Just as often we live in the future. We daydream, we wish, we dread, we fear, we anticipate the future. We spend hours planning and fantasizing. We become so anxious that we need anti-anxiety medications, caffeine or alcohol to function. College students know the way anticipation of the future creates more anxiety than reality itself when their final exams approach. The anxiety they experience ahead of time almost always proves to be far worse than the experience of sitting down to take the exam.

Our thoughts take us into realms that are anything but reality—they are tales we spin about why something occurred in the past or just what will happen in the future. Most of the time the tales have no basis in reality, but they elicit emotions that render us paralyzed. It is never a future event itself that causes anxiety—how can it? It hasn't happened yet! It is our thoughts and feelings surrounding what we think the reality will be that unsettles us.

How aware are we? If we dwelled in the present, not the unreality we so often create by our thoughts, we would be less anxious and more content. We would be more open to seeing those around us and aware of with what they are dealing.

The gospel of Mark reveals the nature and character of Jesus. He is depicted as a man who is fully present. He is able to respond to the needs of people around him. Dozens of times we read that he heals, casts out demons, and feeds the multitudes. When people are hungry, he does not send them away as the disciples suggest, but he sees their acute hunger, has compassion for them, and instructs the disciples to feed them. When a person is ill, he heals them right away.

MISUNDERSTANDING JESUS' MESSAGE

As we look closely at Mark's portrayal of Jesus, we find common understandings of Jesus' purpose are actually misinterpretations, and simply not found here. For example, often we assume Jesus heals, accepts and saves only when a person has professed faith in him as the Messiah. Yet in Mark's gospel, Jesus rarely offers forgiveness or healing in order to reward a sick person for confessing faith in him. More often it is because someone else believes Jesus can heal their friend or family member, such as when Jesus forgives the sins of the paralytic lowered through the roof because he sees the faith of those who bring the man to him. Or he sometimes heals because he wants to make a point to skeptics around him, as when he goes on to heal the same man of his paralysis.[2] Other times he simply asks what a person wants, and grants it for them, with no strings attached.

The consistent point about Jesus' healing is not why he heals, but the fact that a person is in need of healing and he has compassion for them. Huge crowds follow him, and he not only heals them, he insists he and the disciples walk right into the crowds to meet their needs. In the first chapter of Mark alone, we learn that "his fame spread everywhere," and a "whole city was gathered together" and that "people came to him from every quarter."

We may assume Jesus' primary mission is to reveal his identity as the Messiah. Yet, throughout the Gospel of Mark, Jesus does not herald himself as the Savior. He never uses the term Christ, nor Son of God, for himself. Jesus simply goes about his business of healing, feeding and caring. He does not want to be called "the Christ." When, as Mark points out, the demons call him Christ or Son of God, thus recognizing him for who he is—he charges them to be silent. Even when Peter calls him the Christ, Jesus admonishes him not to repeat it.[3]

---

2. Mark 2:3–12.
3. Mark 8:29–30.

Jesus refers to himself as the Son of Man, or as some translate the term anthropos, "the son of humanity."[4] In its generic biblical sense, this phrase may simply mean "human being," or "human being from above," or refers to a human being with divine power.[5] Here, Son of Humanity is used as a title by Jesus, connoting a Divine agent, a title Jesus may have used to refer to himself, or a phrase that may have been turned into a title and attributed to him by the gospel writer.[6]

Jesus does not insist that his disciples go out and proclaim him as the Christ. He tells his disciples to preach the gospel—but that seems mainly to consist of giving them authority to heal demons.[7] Jesus talks to the disciples alone about his identity (which they never quite seem to comprehend—the twelve men closest to him all disappear or deny him in the end). When he sends them out to heal he tells them to go humbly and travel extremely lightly—without extra food, money, or even clothing.[8] Neither does Jesus invite everyone to leave home and follow him. He calls his disciples to follow him, but he doesn't demand the same thing from everybody. Others want to follow Jesus, but he insists that they should go home to their families.[9]

We might be fairly certain that in the gospels, Jesus teaches his disciples to be particularly disciplined in identifying themselves as his followers. Yet, in Mark, Jesus does not even advise his disciples to pray often. He suggests that when they pray, the disciples should forgive anyone they hold something against, and he admonishes

4. Rhoads, et al., *Mark as Story*, 9.

5. See Ezek 2:1, 2:8, and throughout Ezek 3; and Pagels, *Beyond Belief*, 42–43.

6. Crossan, *A Revolutionary Biography*, 50.

7. Mark 3:14–15.

8. Mark 6:8.

9. Mark 5:19.

the hypocrites who pray long prayers for their own glory. Instead he calls his disciples to come away to a quiet place to rest.[10]

Claiming an identity, say, as followers of Christ, is not what is important for the disciples' understanding. In fact, it is just the opposite. Actions matter. A person should "lose her life" in order to gain life,[11] Jesus says. When the disciples are arguing which one of them is best, he says, "If any would be first, he must be last of all and servant of all."[12] Followers should receive him eagerly like a child would, rather than like an adult who wants the best for him or herself. Those who are "first will be last, and the last first."[13] And the greatest commandment is that a person love God with all his heart, and love her neighbor as herself. These are more important than following any ritual or doctrine, or stating any specific beliefs. In a discussion with a Scribe, Jesus sees the Scribe understands this commandment as the most important, and explains that the Scribe is not far from the Kingdom of God.[14] This love, then, exemplifies the character of the reign of God on earth.

We may believe Jesus' primary mission is to die so that believers may know eternal life after death. Yet, as Son of Humanity, a Divine Agent, Jesus is not just preaching about a kingdom of heaven people know in the afterlife. He ushers in what he calls the Kingdom of God on earth. A more apt name today, in a world where we rarely speak of kingdoms, is realm, reign, or rule of God.[15] Mark portrays Jesus as demonstrating what society would be like if this were the true realm of God, a realm Jesus has come

---

10. See Mark 6:31.

11. Mark 8:35.

12. Mark 9:35.

13. Mark 10:31.

14. Mark 12:28–34.

15. Rhoads, et al. use the term "rule of God" in *Mark as Story*, 8. Gustavo Gutiérrez discusses the right of persons in poverty to "existence and the *reign of life*" as he discusses a theology of liberation where the reign of God can be a reality on earth, in *We Drink from Our Own Wells*, 2.

to inaugurate "immediately," a term used frequently in the gospel of Mark.

This is a realm in which no humans are excluded. Recall the woman who is healed when she touches the hem of Jesus' garment. This story is remarkable not only because Jesus is attuned to her touch in the midst of an enormous crowd. It is also remarkable because she is a woman who has had a constant flow of blood for many years. Some Jews at the time would have thought her to be ritually impure, yet Jesus welcomes those whom society shuns as unclean.[16] This woman has already experienced agony in attempt to receive help from physicians, drained her finances, and continues to grow sicker with time. Yet she takes her healing into her own hands, and Jesus responds.[17]

Jesus does not, after all, hang out with the people who are seen as most righteous in society. He is famous for cavorting with tax collectors and sinners. Once I discussed with some college students the question of which people in our time might be regarded the way people within those groups were in the first century. Some replied with expected responses—such as thieves or murderers. One young woman, Megan, offered the insight that it is probably someone that makes able-bodied people very uncomfortable, like a person living with disabilities. And Melissa's response was even more unusual. It was a time when our President's rating in the polls had hit an all-time low due to our continued involvement in the Iraq War, which many were beginning to think was criminal. She said the person Jesus associated with at that moment in history might just be George W. Bush.

Imagine a world in which one who believes in equitable care for all people and continually criticizes the government for exploiting its people, sits down as a friend to eat with an unpopular leader of the free world; or in which all able-bodied persons respect the body and spirit of a person with a disability automatically, without

16. Collins, *Mark*, 284.
17. See St. Clair, *Call and Consequences*, 122–133.

hesitation. This is a vastly different world than the one in which we live.

The Jesus we find in the gospel of Mark is one who has little concern for himself or his reputation. He is not depicted as a Messiah calling others to see and accept him as the Christ. According to some early traditions, Jesus never did claim to be the Messiah. Hence, some claim that Mark is depicting Jesus as correcting claims that he is the Christ, when he tells others not to say so.[18] Others say a major focus of the Gospel of Mark is the failure of the disciples' understanding of the meaning of the passion and of discipleship.[19] Some advocate the position that the disciples are simply not meant to understand.[20]

UNDERSTANDING JESUS' MESSAGE

I propose, instead, that Jesus is ushering in a revolution of compassion. In my reading, Jesus does see himself as the Son of God, the incarnation of God on earth. But his primary purpose is not simply to proclaim this fact. His mission is to bring about a twofold revolution: justice throughout the community and a change of heart to help bring about that new human community. His actions live out the creation of the reign of God, a community of justice. He calls persons around him to participation in this new community. This change of heart is the conversion Jesus calls his followers to embrace. We see that his vision of salvation, and role as Savior in bringing about a new way of compassionate community, is one that is difficult to grasp, even for those who walk with him.

In many ways, Jesus' role is seen more clearly through his actions of care and staying with those who suffer, rather than through his teachings. In Mark's gospel, we see that only a few really understand that Jesus brings a new way to live. It is interesting that

18. Williamson, *Mark*, 13.

19. Perrin, *Resurrection*, 27–31.

20. Achtemeier, *Invitation to Mark*, 23–24.

some commentators note over and over that Jesus' followers do not understand who he is, quoting the words exchanged between Jesus and the disciples, but these same scholars miss the few who do recognize who he is. Apart from an obvious reason they miss it—because the ones who "get it" are women—it may be also because those who understand demonstrate this not with dialogue, but through the actions of their own flesh and body. It is actually remarkable they are even mentioned in the biblical narrative that stems from a more patriarchal culture than ours. Even though they are mentioned, the women are often invisible to our own readings. This may be because in our society we value rationality, too often thought to be masculine work, over the work of the body, such as physical perseverance with one who suffers.

In the fourteenth chapter of Mark, we read of a woman who comes bearing extremely expensive ointment to anoint Jesus. When the disciples protest, he tells them to let her alone. She is the only one in the room who understands it is important to prepare Jesus for his impending burial. She does so not with words or an exclamation of Jesus as the Christ or Messiah or Savior, but with her actions—breaking the expensive alabaster flask of ointment, and pouring it over his head.[21] When Jesus is crucified and the disciples have all fled, we read that the women stay to the end, not recorded as speaking, but present and participating in his suffering. At the cross, women look on, including Mary Magdalene, Mary the mother of James and Joses, Salome, "and also many other women who came up with him to Jerusalem." Mark notes the first two women are again present and see where Jesus' body is lain in the tomb. And all three women are named again, when they come to find the physical body of Jesus in the tomb.[22]

So what does Jesus say one should do? Early on in his ministry he calls listeners specifically to have faith, repent, and come

21. Mark 14:3–9.
22. Mark 15:40–41, 47, 16:1.

after.[23] His call to have faith is not a request to believe a doctrine, the particularities of which are not recorded in the early part of Mark when he addresses the crowds, but rather to have courage to think about the world in new ways.

We have noted Jesus is not asking followers to believe he is the Messiah, but to have faith that he can heal, and that they are worthy of healing. He invites people to walk a new way of faith and vision, to step outside the box. He calls people to repent, or turn from what they are doing and the ways they are thinking, to have courage and not be afraid, and follow the new way he is proposing.[24] Jesus calls followers to a way of radical egalitarianism, of accepting, healing and sharing meals with any and all.[25]

Jesus calls the disciples to community, to attend to the crowd, and to resist the determinism of authorities who perpetuate the system that oppresses the poor.[26] Jesus admonishes those who follow him to have courage to demonstrate humility and compassion for the crowds. He tells his disciples several times, in the face of a large crowd for which he has compassion, "give them something to eat." Jesus reminds the disciples that when they pray they should forgive. Their focus is outward—toward fulfilling the needs of the people.

At the same time, Jesus acknowledges that in order to care for others, they need to be renewed themselves. Jesus encourages the disciples to take care of themselves. As we have mentioned, when the crowds are overwhelming them, he calls his disciples to "come

23. In the *RSV*, "have faith" is translated "believe," and "come after" as "follow."

24. Marcus Borg describes what Jesus meant by "repent" with the phrase: "go beyond the mind that you have," in *Conversations with Scripture*, 31.

25. Crossan uses the term "radical egalitarianism" to describe the message of Jesus, in *Jesus*, 71. Garry Wills also refers to Jesus as a "radical egalitarian," even though the two utilize different methods to interpret who Jesus is, in *What Jesus Meant*, 48.

26. As emphasized by Ched Myers in his political reading of the Gospel of Mark, *Binding the Strong Man*.

away" and to "rest." Having called them to renew themselves for a difficult ministry, at the end of his own ministry, Jesus repeatedly calls to his disciples to participate with him in the suffering he undergoes. As he is about to be arrested by the ruling powers in the Garden of Gethsemane, he asks them to stay awake with him, to sit, watch, and pray.[27]

Sit, watch, pray, and listen. The prominent request Jesus has throughout his ministry to crowds, accusers, and disciples each time he begins to speak is simply to listen. Repeatedly, he refers to the importance of listening. Very often Jesus calls those who have ears to hear to listen. He speaks in parables, and as a result people see but do not perceive, and hear but do not understand. He heals and gives sight to many who are blind. The writer of the gospel of Mark understands the importance of opening one's eyes, and uses it metaphorically when he frames with two healings of blind persons, a section in which Jesus is transfigured on the mountaintop and teaches about what is to come, in attempt to teach the disciples to "see" who he really is.[28]

Jesus opens eyes and ears and calls his followers to come after him and practice a way of radical love, to forgive and to feed. He admonishes them to open their eyes to see whoever is before them in the given moment—not even taking time to change clothes or go out and find food just as they are. He offers that they should take time to have compassion for themselves by coming away and resting. And all this leads to the culmination where followers will learn to listen, watch, and awaken to the world around them.

27. Mark 14:32–42.

28. See Mark 8:22–26 and 10:46–52 and the section in between. Williamson and Achtemeier, among others, discuss this framing in Mark's gospel, in Williamson, *Mark*, 148–200 and Achtemeier, *Invitation to Mark*, 123–158.

THE LIVING CHRIST

There is a discussion between two contrasting paradigms of scriptural interpretation today. One is "belief-centered," a paradigm that focuses on doctrine and the afterlife and what one must do to be saved. The other is an emerging "way-centered" paradigm, that emphasizes Jesus' life and ministry apart from the doctrine developed after his death. [29]

We can acknowledge that the paradigm of belief has a point in its insistence that the Jesus of history is never fully known to us. [30] And we learn from the paradigm of the way that Jesus belongs to a great tradition of wisdom teachers from many religions. But we can go even further than either of these methods. We can recognize it is not just in the Bible that we see Jesus. If we listen and open our eyes as Jesus calls the people around him to do, we will learn to see him everywhere. And we will find teachers in many places to learn how to live as Jesus beckons. Jesus' hospitality will likely show up in places or persons we least expect.

In recent years we changed the name of the campus ministry building where I work from Koinonia House to Interfaith House, to reflect the many groups using our building. Our vision statement became, "a safe place for spiritual development." The Atheist-Agnostic student group is one among dozens of groups that gather in our building. When I invited them some years ago to consider this as their meeting space, I received some criticism from a few Christian sponsors whether this group should be welcome in our building. Contrast this attitude with that of the students themselves. For soon, it came to my attention that several members of a conservative Christian organization on campus routinely showed up at weekly meetings, and argued philosophy and theology with the Atheist and Agnostic students. Concerned that the students

---

29. Borg outlines these two paradigms for understanding Jesus, in *Jesus*, 14–26.

30. Wills, *What Jesus Meant*, xxvi.

felt safe to express their viewpoints and that the guests might be deterring honest discussion; I asked the president of the Atheist-Agnostic student group if this was also his concern. His reply was, "Oh, no, anyone is welcome to our meetings!"

Our sources for where we might see the Spirit of Jesus are almost infinite. *The Gospel of Thomas*, hidden for several thousand years in an earthen jar in Nag Hammadi, Egypt, is a simple collection of Jesus' sayings. Written by early followers of Jesus, called Gnostic Christians, it is believed to be authentic and even to predate the Gospel of Mark.[31] Listen to what Jesus says, according to this gospel, about where he is found:

> Split a piece of wood,
> and I am there.
> Pick up a stone,
> and you will find me there.[32]

We might even say we can find the Living Christ wherever we see this Spirit of welcome, forgiveness, healing and compassion. Many understand the Presence of God to be the Living Christ, manifest in the world. The gospel of Mark ends with the death of Jesus on the cross and the empty tomb. [33] In chapters fifteen and sixteen, we learn the story told among Jesus' early followers, that after he is killed, the women who are Jesus' close friends come to his tomb and find it empty. There they encounter a young man dressed in a white robe, who tells them that Jesus of Nazareth is risen. They are instructed to tell his disciples, and to go to Galilee, where they will see him. We read that they react with astonishment and flee.

---

31. Pagels, *Gnostic Gospels*, xvii. Crossan points out there are significant parallels between the material in this newly discovered work with material in Mark's Gospel, in *Birth of Christianity*, 248–49.

32. *The Gospel of Thomas*, Saying 75, in Meyer, *Secret Teachings*, 33.

33. The last verses in Mark, 16:9–20, in which Jesus heralds the resurrection after his death, are believed to have been added several centuries later, perhaps when the readers felt a need to understand his life in light of his death. See, for example, Williamson, *Mark*, 7.

The Living Christ is the form and title the Presence of the Divine takes on for Christians.[34] In further stories from the epistles and the other three gospels, we find that Jesus' followers come to believe he has defied death and been resurrected. They see Jesus with their own eyes, talk with him, and eat with him. Soon after, Jesus himself is no longer seen, but the actions he calls people to and the way he calls them to live are apparent, as early Christians continue to live in community and care for one another, confirmed within the communities to whom the apostle Paul writes. Evidence of Jesus in New Testament times, and today where such caring community exists, is manifest in the world. Jesus lives.

We see the Presence of Christ all around, as well as within us, when we open our eyes. As we live fully in the present, followers of this way experience deep peace within this Living Presence. We know ourselves completely and fully accepted, just as Jesus unconditionally accepted even the worst sinners around him when he walked upon the earth. We participate in the work of Christ, as his hands, feet and body—bringing peace not only within but around us, to a world in which suffering and death never have the last word.

34. Norman Perrin summarizes his interpretation of the death and resurrection of Jesus in Mark's understanding this way: "For me to say 'Jesus is risen!' in Markan terms means to say that I experience Jesus as ultimacy in the historicality of my everyday, and that that experience transforms my everydayness as Mark expected the coming of Jesus as Son of man to transform the world," in *Resurrection*, 38.

2

Understanding God

JESUS DWELLS consciously in the Presence of God. We rarely see God as a character in Mark's gospel (twice, God's voice is heard), but we recognize Jesus' deep relationship with God.[1] Jesus often escapes to a quiet place to pray, and at the end of his life he addresses God like all of us do as humans at some point in our lives when we can't figure out "Why me?" He addresses God with the term Abba (Father) as he sits in the garden of Gethsemane. This is Jesus' own intimate prayer, not an admonition that this is the only way to address God (in fact, it almost feels as if we're eavesdropping upon this prayer—as no one seems to be within his hearing at the time).[2] He talks about the need for prayer in healing certain kinds of diseases, but we do not hear his actual words of prayer—knowing the Presence of God just seems to be part of who Jesus is.[3]

If a life of faith means dwelling in a way that one is simply infused and surrounded by and one with that Presence, our language fails us. What metaphor for, or image of God, can fully characterize the Presence that is All? Any language we use for God is inadequate, because it is a human construct. Islamic recitations repeat that God is beyond anything or anyone humans can define, such as "Limitless is He in His glory, and sublimely exalted above anything that men may devise by way of definition . . . No human

---

1. We read of a voice "from heaven" and "out of the cloud," in Mark 1:11 and 9:7.

2. Mark 14:36.

3. Mark 9:29.

vision can encompass Him, whereas He encompasses all human vision: for He alone is unfathomable, all-aware."[4]

The Jewish tradition embodies this as well, when it insists that the name of G—d never be spoken. In the Hebrew, it is written without vowels, and therefore not pronounceable, as YHWH. The Divine can also described in Judaism as "via negationis," meaning humans can never claim adequately what this Divine is, only what it is not.[5]

Native American cultures describe this Great Mystery in a variety of ways. The Great Mystery is also a "void." God is not a thing, but events with neither end nor beginning, that "simply are always and everywhere." The Lakota describe God as movement, sometimes named "Sky that Moves."[6]

In spite of its many names for God, Hinduism too understands that the most accurate description of the Infinite and Unsearchable is "neti . . . neti," meaning, "not this . . . not this."[7] The Bhagavadgita contains eloquent descriptions of the Supreme God as essentially indefinable. In a short section from one such longer passage, the "All, The Uncreated" is described this way:

> Not Form, nor the Unformed; yet both—and more; . . .
> He is within all beings—and without—
> Motionless, yet still moving; not discerned
> For subtlety of instant presence; close
> To all, to each; yet measurelessly far!
> Not manifold, and yet subsisting still
> In all which lives . . .[8]

---

4. Asad, Qur'an, 6:100, 103. In many other verses God is described to be far beyond what can be attributed by humans, such as "Celebrated then be the praise of Allah, the Lord of the throne, above what they ascribe!" Qur'an 21:22, in Palmer, Koran, 294.

5. Heschel, Sabbath, 15.

6. Allen Grandmothers of the Light, 107–8.

7. Smith, World's Religions, 47.

8. Arnold, Bhagavadgita, 69.

On September 19, 2001, shortly after the tragic destruction of the Twin Towers in New York City, students held the first of a series of interfaith dialogues that continued throughout the year at our campus ministry. Panel members comprised of the presidents of various religious student organizations were each asked to answer several questions, including, "How do you describe God?" Following the discussion, Malcolm said to me, "After the dialogue, Rizzal and I walked up to one another, and we were speechless. It was a powerful dialogue. I mean, when you ask four students of various faiths to describe God, and they all answer, essentially, that 'God is indescribable'—that is amazing."

We need not only to come up with a new way to speak of the Divine, but a radically new way to conceptualize It. If we simply shift our language, we are transferring our images and metaphors, rather than gaining a whole new awareness of the Sacred.

METAPHORS FOR GOD

I learned how metaphors of God are often really idols some years ago, as a woman in ministry. I was privileged to take one of the first courses, if not the first, at my seminary on the emerging feminist theology in the late 1970s. We read Mary Daly's startling statement that "if God is male, then the male is God."[9] We searched the Scriptures for female metaphors and attributes of God—and found dozens.

In the Book of Proverbs, we find Wisdom, or the Greek feminine term Sophia, who was with God upon creation. Jesus compares himself to a mother hen who would protect her baby chicks.[10] But one of my favorite characterizations where I see the feminine in the Divine comes from Genesis 3.[11] Adam, Eve and the

9. Daly, *Beyond God the Father*, 19.

10. Prov 3:19; Matt 23:37; Luke 13:34.

11. Today, we recognize what has traditionally been called feminine, or tender motherly behavior, in both Mothers and Fathers, enabling us to refer to God as Nurturing Parent, or Mother or Father interchangeably. The point

snake have just been properly rebuked for their disobedience. God then acts like a mother or nurturing parent who has just scolded her kids, then taking pity on them as she sees that they feel bad asks if they would like something to eat, or to go to the mall, perhaps. After delivering a smoldering scolding and threatening them with no less than eternal consequences for their behavior, God takes pity on Eve and Adam who are feeling embarrassed now that they realize they are naked, and in a tender moment in scripture, She clothes them.[12]

Another example is found in the story of Noah and the Ark. When Noah builds an ark against all human logic, and succeeds somehow at getting a pair of every species of animal into the ark along with him and his family, God shows up. God acts like a mother or nurturing parent who, knowing her child has had a long and emotional day, has put the child to bed and sung a lullaby to help him or her sleep, then tiptoes out the door and closes it behind to shut out all the problems of the world. Once all the animals and Noah's family are safely tucked inside with Noah, like that parent, She safely shuts them in.[13]

Yet, when my colleagues and I became pastors of churches and introduced the idea that perhaps God could be referred to as Mother as well as Father (especially when we did so by invoking God the Mother at the beginning of the Lord's Prayer)—there was no question by the reaction of congregations and fellow pastors that we were tried and true heretics. God the Father is Absolute in the Christian theology of most churches, still today. And any metaphor for God that is Absolute, we learned from Moses way back in Exodus, is an idol.

---

is that when God acts this way, God can be referred to as Mother as easily and accurately as referring to God as Father.

12. Gen 3:21.

13. Gen 7:16.

GOD AS PRESENCE

If we are to come to know God, then, we have to drop our idols and absolute doctrines and theologies, and simply be open to Presence, here and now. We learn from Moses, the only one in the Bible brave enough to confront God with the question of what he should say when others ask who sent him to them, and to actually get an answer. God replies to Moses that he should say this to anyone who asks who sent him: "I Am Who I Am."[14] "Am" is a derivative of the word "is." God Is. Anything that attempts to define God beyond pure presence, reality, isness, Being itself, then, is metaphor. And any time a metaphor is held to be the only way to define God, it is idolatry.

Note Jesus' response to the high priest's question, "Are you the Christ?" He echoes God's response to Moses when asked God's name, by beginning his reply simply, "I am."[15]

If we are to use a word such as Presence or Being instead of God or Divine, then, what is this other than just a change in our language? What shift occurs in our understanding of Presence? First, Presence and Being are real only in this very moment. What was a day or year ago no longer is—it is only memory. What will be tomorrow is not yet—except in our imagination and our anticipation. This is not some eternal Thing or Father that is making the world happen or causing the next event in our lives. This is the world itself, the very life breath of the present moment. This is not a concept at all—it just Is.

Second, we, too, dwell only in the present—in a moment we could cease to breathe, and a moment ago we were having thoughts or feelings that have now faded. There is only now. It is amazing to realize that our very presence, our very life, our very breath, our very being, is at One with the Presence of Life and Being itself.

14. Exod 3:14.
15. Mark 14:62.

I once participated in a Friday evening service held by our local Jewish community. At one point, the guest rabbi asked the congregation to speak the name of God. The room was silent. As we have noted, the name of God is simply not spoken out loud. "Just whisper it, then," she said. Still no response. "Ok, breathe it," she finally suggested. "Inhale *Yah* and exhale *weh*." The name of the Divine is the Breath of Life.

Not long after, a friend suggested to me that if you are going to pray to God using the Arabic name, don't forget to say the "Ah." Allahhhhh. The name of the Divine is the Breath of Life. In addition, Brahman, the Sanskrit name for God, is derived in part from "br," meaning "to breathe."[16] The Bhagavadgita compares the "Ultimate…like to th' ethereal air, pervading all."[17]

These are only a fraction of the references in spiritual texts of the connection between the Supreme Being and breath, or air. We noted the Lakota name the Great Mystery to be "Spirit that Moves." Another Lakota name for this is "Wind."[18]

Omid Safi emphasizes the intrinsic worth of every human being, as in the Qur'an God states in two distinct passages, "I breathed into humanity something of My own spirit."[19] Humans are formed out of the very Breath of God. In the Hebrew story of the creation of Adam, as it is told in the book of Genesis, when God forms the human out of the earth, God breathes into the human's nostrils *nephesh*, the breath of life. The breath of life is also manifested in the term *ruah*, also meaning spirit, or air as breath or wind. And the Hebrew term *'adam* is drawn from *'adama*, the earth.[20] Early Hebrew people understood every human creature is birthed from the earth, and given life, spirit and breath through the Breath of the Creator.

16. Smith, *World's Religions*, 47.

17. Arnold, *Bhagavadgita*, 71.

18. Allen, *Grandmothers of the Light*, 108.

19. Qur'an 15:29; 38:72. Translation by Safi, *Progressive Muslims*, 3, 27.

20. See notes in *The New Jerusalem Bible* on Gen 2:7, 6:17.

This is a Presence we do not speak only of believing in, but is the very Breath we breathe. It is One we draw life from and dwell and are enveloped within. When she reached her nineties, my friend Pauline Thompson often quoted Carl Jung in her own writing, saying Jung claimed, "I don't believe in God, I know."[21] This is a Presence we just know—that is in and through and around us every moment of every day. This is a Presence we are surrounded by and live unceasingly within, echoing the Apostle Paul's admonition to the Thessalonians, that they pray "constantly," or without ceasing.[22]

It is the work of humans to awaken to Presence. This wisdom is found at the heart of Buddhism. The Buddha replied when asked whether he was a god, an angel or a saint, "No, I am awake."[23] Hindu text encourages: "Who have the eyes to see . . . Enlightened, they perceive that Spirit in themselves . . ."[24] By practicing waking up, by being aware, we know Presence. Recall Jesus' request to the disciples in the Garden of Gethsemane, which they ignored three times, to stay awake with him.

IMAGES OF GOD

Faith is not a product, the endpoint being belief in a particular understanding of God, but a process. Faith development theory holds that as people mature in faith, their image of God shifts. This theory emerges from psychological moral development theories. I have some difficulty with these stages, as they make faith development seem like a straight line, and imply that every person follows the same linear trajectory.[25] Our theology is more compatible with

---

21. Stearns, *Writing Pauline*, 80.

22. I Thess 5:17.

23. Smith, *World's Religions*, 59.

24. Arnold, *Bhagavadgita*, 79.

25. James Fowler and Sam Keen build upon the work in moral development of such thinkers as Jean Piaget and Lawrence Kohlberg, who saw these stages as "sequential, hierarchical, invariant, and universal," in *Life Maps*, 29.

an ethic of care and compassion, than one insisting upon fixed, hierarchical notions of morality and principle.[26] Our lives are impermanent, centered in presence, and always lived within the context of communities of care, rather than formed along a pre-planned, vertical ladder of moral development.

However, an understanding of faith development outlining ways different people conceptualize the Divine in the world, is useful as it has been outlined by Scotty McLennan. Just as we develop physically, intellectually and morally, we develop spiritually. McLennan describes the faith of many college students, and of a large percentage of adults, as having an understanding of faith he terms "Dependent."[27] Here, we understand God to be a parental figure, upon whom we are dependent and from whom we receive reprimands and blessings.

I often hear college students, at a time when many find themselves away from home for the first time, explain that they have discovered they don't believe in God anymore. It may be, instead, that they indeed believe in God, but in a parental image in God. They don't attend church because they figure, just the way they might with their own parents, that if they are not around God the Father when they engage in experimental behavior, then He can't see them either.

What can occur when they are given a space and permission in which to question the image of God that doesn't work for them anymore (the one that tells them what they should do or not do), is college students, and the rest of us, grow into a more "Independent" type of faith. One of the most rewarding repeated experiences in campus ministry is the moment during a conversation when a student suddenly understands that he can think for

26. See Carol Gilligan's criticism of these theories as masculine in scope, advocating instead caring within the context of relationships as a basis for ethical theory, in her ground-breaking work, *In a Different Voice*. See Emilie Townes, *Breaking the Fine Rain*, for a fully developed Womanist Ethic of Care.

27. McLennan, *Finding Your Religion*, 21–25.

himself. Such as, when he realizes an image of God that left him feeling inadequate or guilty is not the only way to understand God. Or with another student, when she feels embraced and accepted just as she is, or catches a glimpse of a mystery far beyond definitions and boundaries for the first time.

With this understanding, God is seen as more like Spirit, even distant. Eventually, we embrace an Interdependence, where we understand the Divine as infinite and immense, yet paradoxically also intimate and integral within everyday life. Many elders in my life demonstrate this balance and depth within their lives.

Finally, McLennan suggests, there are those exceptional spiritual people who come to a place of absolute acceptance and love for all humanity, with an all-encompassing understanding of God.[28] We can imagine Jesus, offering healing to any in need, demonstrates this enormous faith. We see it in others as well, persons who are deeply grounded in their own faith, but do not expect everyone else to be a certain way in order to acknowledge and love them. Many who have seen him have noted the deep humility of the Dalai Lama, for example, noting the most remarkable thing about him is how he treats everyone equally.[29] The Dalai Lama himself writes:

> I travel to many places around the world, and whenever I speak to people, I do so with the feeling that I am a member of their own family. Although we may be meeting for the first time, I accept everyone as a friend.[30]

Thich Nhat Hanh claims that when he met Martin Luther King, Jr., he knew he was in the presence of a holy person.[31] Many have confirmed feeling when in his very presence, the love and passion for justice King had for all of humanity. These are but a few examples—we could go on to discuss the experience people

---

28. See chapter on "Opening," McLennan, *Finding Your Religion*, 9–32.

29. Brach, *Radical Acceptance*, 232.

30. Dalai Lama, *How to Practice*, 1.

31. Nhat Hanh, *Living Buddha*, 5–6.

have had of meeting Mother Teresa and others. These persons are deeply grounded within their own religious tradition, yet express a genuine love for all people.

UNDERSTANDING GOD'S WILL

Erasing all metaphors for God is not the point, as they do bring meaning to many believers. Instead, we know these are always partial, and we live in a much larger Presence within Life and Being, than our specific metaphors for the Divine can even come close to portraying. While believing "it is in God's hands" is comforting, it has also created tremendous theological conflict between opposing notions of human free will and God's will. If God knows best, then how do we have free will—it would seem there is just one right pathway for us to take. This theology views God in an exclusively anthropomorphic way—that is, it attributes human qualities to God.

Believing there is just one life path for us, determined ahead of time by God, can cause us to deny our human desires and gifts in order to embrace a more disciplined path (which is surely the one God has planned for us, if we do His will). What can result, and has for some, is a kind of war between our own inner wisdom, or what we might know deep down to be right for ourselves, and an outer understanding of the disciplined Christian life. What can result is, frankly, a tormented and unhappy life.

We are who we are. We are human, with all our desires and mistakes and misunderstandings. This does not mean we would necessarily choose to do just anything we want anytime. For in community, we live with compassion, forgiveness, love and do not judge ourselves or one another, if we choose to treat people the way Jesus treated them. We are humans and trying to learn compassion for others and discover our authentic selves, can become our guide for action, instead of simply following disciplinary rules that alienate us from our true selves.

Rather than solely thinking about an anthropomorphic Father/Mother who has things all planned out for us, we can understand ourselves as living fully in the Presence of Being Itself. We are one with the Sacred as our lives move within the realm of the sacred and meaningful. Jewish, Christian and Sufi understandings offer correctives for the common practice of creating God in the image of the human Father or Mother. Just the opposite— humans are created in the image of God. Sufism sees the essential human Self as a reflection of Spirit, or God.[32] And in Genesis we read that God said, "Let us make humankind in our image, after our likeness."[33]

Note the notion of Divine inspiration of scripture becomes a moot point when we understand there is, in actuality, no anthropomorphic God moving the hand of the writer or any human being. When we read about this type of God, we know it is simply a way for us as humans to get a handle on the character of Being. It is always a metaphor. There is no God moving history in human terms—there is simply Being itself. Further, "I Am" is not an anthropomorphic God making things happen in a life from one moment to the next. There is no God's will for me because there is no God who is separate from my very being and Life everywhere. There is only the present and learning to live, awake to the synchronous moments in life and aware of the meaning they bring to my life.

I met Susan in the airport as we awaited our respective flights home after attending a conference on Christian worship. She told me she recently followed God's lead when her advertising business was having trouble due to the economy, as she began to downsize and prepare to move. She considered becoming a minister, and was accepted to a prestigious eastern seminary. Deep down, however, the move didn't feel quite right. Soon she met a new partner, and ended up moving so they could be together, putting seminary

---

32. Helminski, *Living Presence*, 7.
33. Gen 1:26, as translated in Trible, *God and the Rhetoric*, 13.

on hold for the time being. She said she knew that all along, God had that plan ready for her, and her preparation to move was just for a different purpose than she originally understood.

I was moved by Susan's story and her willingness to be open to change and to new opportunity that appeared in the present moment. We might not agree that there is a God out there with a plan all laid out for her life. I would put it another way, saying that when we are open to our inner voice and the present, we are in tune and alive in Presence and experience synchronicity in our lives.[34]

Of course we use the language of metaphor in prayer and conversation, just as Jesus did, when we say Father or Mother or Creator God. We also use the language of God's will at times. I use various names for God as a minister, because I know how powerful these metaphors are in the life of a person who is ill in a hospital bed, or sitting in a church pew on Sunday morning. I know we need to gather our thoughts and direct them to one far greater than ourselves, and images help us to do so. The words of prayer are not empty words—they are filled with meaning and power. But every time we use a name to address Presence, we know it is never adequate, and only a symbol of the Presence in which we dwell.

Finally, it may be that where we come to know Presence and Being in an even deeper way is when we sit, watch and listen in silence. We often spend so much time trying to discern God's will we miss the Presence that is here and now.

HOLINESS IN TIME

If we set aside the idea of a God who makes things happen in our lives, versus a Presence in which we dwell, we move into the realm of the eternal and a new understanding of time. Time as we know it takes on a sacred quality. Our bodies, minds, and emotions tie us to time as we age. But our spiritual enlightenment occurs as we

---

34. See Chapter 6, "Discovering the Self," for more on "synchronicity."

learn to stop being held in bondage to time, and live deeply in the present. Eternal life is living in Presence, fully and deeply.

Abraham Heschel writes: "There is a realm of time where the goal is not to have but to be, not to own but to give, not to control but to share, not to subdue but to be in accord."[35] In his beautiful, now classic work on honoring the Jewish Sabbath, Heschel differentiates between living in the realm of space, which includes things such as work and the material accumulation of objects; and time, wherein we find "holiness." He notes how the first entity declared holy in the Bible is time, when God declares the seventh day one of rest.

Another way to conceptualize this experience of Presence is as one of being outside time as we normally know it, or having a sense of timelessness. While taking a week-long retreat during which I pondered many of the themes that would end up in this book, I wrestled with the question, "Who are you, Christ?" Finally, toward the end of the week, I received the answer: "Timeless." Carl Jung describes his struggles with God, writing that when he was alone with God, "I was outside time; I belonged to the centuries . . ."[36]

We have all had experiences when "time stood still," or we felt suspended in time. We have been caught in the holiness of time. In my spiritual biography of Pauline E. Thompson, my friend and elder mentor, I describe such an experience. Throughout my study of her life, I entered Pauline's world as it existed in her tenth decade of life, where philosophizing, theorizing, and just simply being took precedence over the clock:

> I recall one day arriving at Pauline's doorstep near lunchtime, bringing lunch to share from a local deli so she would not need to dig out one of the many meals-on-wheels she had stashed into her refrigerator. We sat at Pauline's old kitchen table, and I turned on my tape recorder and began our interview. The air soon filled with Pauline's stories, remarkably varied, yet all connected in some way . . . Carrying steaming

35. Heschel, *Sabbath*, 3.
36. Jung, *Memories*, 48.

cups of Pauline's favorite ginseng tea we retired to the worn, brown couch in the living room, talking until the light grew a pale gray as the sun slipped below the horizon. . . . I was quite startled when I glanced at my watch and realized not one, as I had thought, but five hours had elapsed. Time was temporarily suspended as I entered Pauline's world of story, presence, and thought.[37]

As we can experience in relationships, on the journey of faith we dwell deeply in holy time, in the Presence of Being and Life. We move into a new dimension of mystery and time. Taking Sabbath for a Jewish family is an invitation, "to share what is eternal in time, to turn from the results of creation to the mystery of creation; from the world of creation to the creation of the world."[38] We enter into the Presence of the one who offers us true compassion and in whom we learn to live in the absolute present, to be truly alive and awake, to listen, watch and sit.

37. Stearns, *Writing Pauline*, xvii.

38. Heschel, *Sabbath*, 10.

3

Living in the Present

JESUS DEMONSTRATES living deeply in the present. There are a rich variety of teachers from whom we can learn what it means to live this way.

Mystics throughout the history of Christianity, and contemporary Christian monastics have discovered how to live in Presence. Records of Christian mystics go back hundreds of years. Some pray with techniques such as lectio divina, focusing on the words of script ure for meditation and prayer. Others pray the Jesus Prayer, or develop the method of Contemplative Prayer.[1] One main attribute that sets these practitioners apart from the rest of us is the anchoring of all of life in various forms of repeated daily prayer. Jesus goes away by himself to pray after meeting large crowds. He invites his disciples to join him in going to a lonely place, to rest awhile. Living a life of prayer is the way we might phrase in more traditional language the experience of going away to a place apart to sit in Presence, about which people in contemporary as well as past religious orders have much to teach us.

"Prayer is not something we do," said Sister Mary Kay, a Benedictine sister, "prayer is God's act." As we sat with a cup of coffee one evening in her monastery dining room, I asked the monastery's former prioress to tell me about prayer. She explained to me that if you get serious about prayer, several things will occur.

1. On "lectio divina," see Pennington, *Centering Prayer*, 30–31. Narratives on the origins of centering prayer from the lives of Christian mystics can be found in chapters 2 and 3 of Pennington; and in chapter 3 of Keating, *Open Mind*.

"First, you will face yourself in a new way," she replied, then added, "Second, you will change. You will have to give up things you've been holding onto." She continued, "Third, if you get serious about prayer, you will have to do the works of justice."

Prayer is something God does. That in itself went against what I knew about prayer. Secondly, that prayer has to do with learning about ourselves, and letting go of those things we cling to, were also new ideas for me. But that prayer has to do with justice? I was startled. Growing up, that's not what I learned. I learned that prayer was talking to God, asking for the things I wanted first, then asking forgiveness for the things I felt bad about (or maybe the other way around). And if I didn't get everything I wanted, well, I had to assume God knew better and I didn't really need those things. This is the God of what should be—the God who knows better, and the God who expects me to be different than I am.

But what Sister Mary Kay describes is a new way altogether. If prayer is something God does, it genuinely sounds like a way to rest awhile, as Jesus said. Just rest, relax into the experience. God does the rest. How do we learn to let go of our control, even of our prayers, and simply rest in Presence?

We start by going away to a "lonely" or quiet place. To just sit. Watch. Listen. Without agenda; without control; without our own ideas of what will happen. The first thing that will happen if we take this new prayer, this new listening seriously, is that we will see ourselves in a whole new way. We will see who we really are. Not our idea of how pious or faithful we think we should be. But who we are—anxieties, habits, blemishes, talents and blessings—all of it.

RADICAL ACCEPTANCE

This is radical acceptance. This is coming to see and accept ourselves unconditionally. This is coming to see what is—without an agenda to change or judge. We don't look at ourselves so we can chastise ourselves or feel guilty. When we face ourselves, it is frightening—as any who have engaged in counseling, therapy, or serious meditation know. What we find is not necessarily what we want to see. But it is what is—it is who we are. When we take our spiritual journey seriously, we learn what forgiveness really means—we learn to forgive ourselves. We learn about Presence with us here and now—with our imperfect, broken, sometimes even despicable self. Spiritual teacher Tara Brach makes clear "radical acceptance" of oneself is the first step on an inward journey to come to know wholeness, kindness and love.[2] Or we might use the term "radical humility." This humility is never self-deprecating, but includes a humble and tender acceptance of our reality, as we enter a state of blessedness and being.[3]

If we go away to sit in a quiet place and are confronted with our thoughts and feelings, unedited, and if we let go of our control—we will change. We may even begin to let go of things we think are so essential to ourselves and our lives.

Those of us who call ourselves Christians too often recognize briefly that we have sinned, then insist on moving on to the feeling of knowing forgiveness and being blessed as one of the chosen forgiven. When I accepted Christ into my heart as a young teenager, my youth group leaders made it clear it was important I always appeared to be joyful in Christ (I knew that just by looking at them—they were obviously secure in their faith and showed that joy to the world). I knew that if I really had faith, the world would see it—I would be a nice person to everyone around me. That quick move from guilt to niceness is not only cheap grace, it is ignoring reality. If our goal is just to appear happy then this journey isn't about knowing Something Greater than ourselves or a better world or deep peace within—it is misguidedly focused on ourselves, and others' perceptions of us.

2. See Brach, *Radical Acceptance*.

3. Mirabai Starr uses the term "radical humility" to describe St. John of the Cross' understanding of humility, in her Introduction to St. John of the Cross, *Dark Night*, 10.

REPENTANCE AND CONVERSION

Joan Chittister calls for a new "spirituality of struggle" for a world and individual lives encountering struggle we cannot escape. She describes our individual lives and our communal existence as filled with struggle, so that each of us will face a time where we will "have to choose sometime, someway, between giving up and growing stronger" in our lives.[4] She identifies the first gift of struggle as an invitation to conversion.

Jesus calls people to conversion—to a whole new way of understanding. Conversion is not just an immediate process, or a one-time occurrence, after which we are cleansed and permanently changed. Those who are spiritual people are open to such change, and will learn from unwanted, involuntary change. Our spirituality teaches us that no struggle leaves us unchanged. It can lead to acceptance, and a change in heart. This is a heart filled with forgiveness. This conversion that occurs through prayer leads us to do justice, as described by Sister Mary Kay. Conversion begins with solitude, which moves us toward a profound community life, where we see the need for justice, and the plight of real humans in need in our world.[5]

Deep change—this is what Jesus means by repentance. He urges his disciples to go and preach that humans can repent.[6] We *can* change. We are not stuck with the same mistakes we made before. But that change begins with absolute acceptance of who we are right now, the kind of acceptance Jesus shows everyone who comes into his presence. We are who we are, and staying present with ourselves within a profoundly accepting Presence is where we begin to be gentle with ourselves, and to give ourselves the care

4. Chittister, *Scarred by Struggle*, 2.

5. Gustavo Gutiérrez says, "Conversion entails a break with a previous situation in which for one or another reason solidarity with the poor either did not exist or existed only as a possibility," in *We Drink from Our Own Wells*, 101. See also chapter 6 and p. 131–135.

6. Mark 6:12.

we deserve. We begin by taking the luxury of time out and sitting in a quiet place.

SILENT PRAYER AND MEDITATION

The practice of going away to a quiet place to learn to live in Presence has long been practiced within Christianity. St. John of the Cross discusses prayer as solitude, in which God speaks to the heart. This prayer is about listening, rather than talking. His friend and mentor, Teresa of Avila, describes what she calls the "Prayer of the Quiet." This prayer is a gentle experience of listening. She describes sitting in this prayer as entering your interior castle. Imagine, she poses, your senses and faculties have for a time gone outside, where they are not appreciated for their beauty. Allowing them back inside is the place where one will find God, by drawing one's attention lovingly inward.[7]

In some religions, silent meditation has not just been the practice of mystics marginalized by mainstream theology, and hence has been more central and much more fully developed. Many religious paths focus on the importance of present awareness. This awareness is cultivated by practitioners in a Buddhist sangha, a Taoist hermitage, or a Hindu ashram. And while some may imagine the goal of meditation is to reach an enlightened state of nirvana, many teachers within these traditions will say the task is rather to be awake, aware, and to come to know one's self fully here and now. A Russian Orthodox teacher writes, "It is essential to learn how to wake up," and finds this awakening occurs when one takes time for silence.[8] A Trappist monk discusses these practices within various religious traditions, and notes that Christian

---

7. See chapter on the "Fourth Dwelling," which is the "Prayer of the Quiet" in Teresa of Avila, *The Interior Castle*, 96–114. See a discussion of the importance of the influence of St. John and St. Teresa for silent prayer in Pennington, *Centering Prayer*, 47–50.

8. Clément, *Taizé*, 54.

contemplation is unique in that the awareness developed is one of participation in the distinct "Being of God, Who is 'in us.'"[9]

When we take time out, we become aware not only of ourselves, but our connectedness. Recently, my friend asked me to pray for something specific going on in his life. I told him if I was to be honest I needed to confess to him that in my daily prayer, I don't pray the way he thinks I do. I sit in what I believe to be Presence, in the present itself, for a half hour each day. But I don't speak. Prayer for me is beyond words. "So when I ask you to pray for me, you don't use words but simply lift me before God?" he asked. Christians within the Society of Friends would call this "holding him in the light," a type of prayer they have practiced for many years. Sitting in silence opens our hearts to others.

Contemplative prayer, or meditation as it emerges from various religious traditions, is the obvious way to learn to be in Presence; to be in the radical present. It is clearly worth practicing, but undoubtedly not for everyone. A student and friend of mine once asked me if I thought he should learn to meditate. He was a teacher of martial arts, and soon after I had the opportunity to watch him and some of his students. As I observed their movements marked by balance and precision, it seemed clear to me he was already immersed in the present focus one gains from meditation. I told him later that it appeared to me his practice of the martial arts was much the same as meditation: disciplined, measured, and extremely in the present. Long distance runners, practitioners of yoga and persons who engage in other forms of physical discipline tell me they similarly experience being in the present.[10]

The point is to learn to live here and now. As we drove an hour and a half to the airport after he gave a symposium my orga-

9. Merton, *The Inner Experience*, 11.

10. St. Teresa of Avila acknowledges that there are persons for whom a contemplative life is unsuitable, and writes to these: "Maybe God wants you to worship him with an active life," in *Interior Castle*, 113.

nization sponsored, I discussed with Omid Safi, Sufi practitioner and scholar of Islam, how to practice knowing God in the Present. As he spoke, we gazed around us at the beautiful colors painting the Spokane valley. It was autumn, and the leaves displayed the colors of burning embers, yellow squash and pumpkin. Color, Safi noted, makes him mindful of the character of God. And friend-ship, we both noted—spending rich time sharing with friends an-chors us deeply in the present moment. One of my good friends, Libby, tells me she takes a walk to do an errand each day over the noon hour, and for just ten minutes stops thinking about work and simply listens and observes. Both my conversations through the years with her and other close friends over lunch or dinner, and her time walking over the noon hour, are experiences of being in the present.

THE GIFT OF PAUSING

Many religious people understand the importance of pausing throughout the day. Millions of Muslims structure their days around pausing five times daily for prayer. When we pause, we dwell in holy time, bringing the reality and beauty of the present to life.

Spiritual teachers talk about creating a space within, or hav-ing an open heart, or pausing, and others, like Jesus, about sit-ting and listening. When we take time out to listen and to pause a whole new world opens up—one that has been here all along. We already have spaciousness within—we simply do not pay attention to it. When we pause to look around us, we see what is, and that we were previously unaware of.

Olivier Clément describes the need to awaken "the spaces of the heart." He explains this is why the French community of Taizé is so effective and draws thousands of young people to its small village each week throughout the year. There, a community of brothers live a monastic life, and people join them weekly to experience for just one week their simple, present life. The community is dedicated to teaching young people about reconciliation among Christians, living in simplicity, and developing compassion for the poor throughout the world. I once asked Brother John of Taizé how the brothers first went about inviting the young people and encouraging them to come. He said they didn't. Instead, the young people just began to come. Then, the brothers discovered the need for new ways to communicate the mystery of Christ with all these youth in a short time.

At Taizé, the heart is awakened through liturgy and repetition that does not force doctrine, but conveys a sense of mystery—sung in languages from around the world. All who enter the Church of the Reconciliation are invited to what Clément terms "inhabited" silence. Visitors learn how to listen, and in doing so, are invited to wake up.[11]

I asked a friend, an accomplished painter and sculptor, what it is that makes a visual artist. He suggested to me that while the rest of us see the objects before us, an artist sees the spaces between the objects. It is the space, not the things, that enables them to see and portray reality in a way many of us do not. And in doing so, they facilitate seeing for the rest of us, when we view their art. Musicians know that hitting the right notes can be learned by many people, but the rhythm and rests between each note create music. Pausing brings harmony within us, as we listen in the spaces between our cluttered thoughts.

PRACTICING KINDNESS TO OURSELVES

For those who are physically able and interested, silent prayer and meditation offer a welcome moment of reality, pausing, and discovering the spaciousness of presence. I was first introduced to meditation over thirty years ago. Off and on through the years I have studied different techniques and tried them for a period of

11. Clément, *Taizé*, 53.

time. But always it was a struggle. I couldn't concentrate enough, my thoughts kept getting in the way, or I was feeling too depressed, or I was physically uncomfortable. Most of the time I just couldn't fit meditation or silent prayer into my busy schedule. When I tried, I dreaded that time to sit down each day because I could never do it just right.

Even today, I will sit down and prepare to just "be"—and twenty to forty minutes might go by before I am aware that I have even been thinking. I plan my day's activities, the dinner menu and even a whole vacation! Many versions of chapters for this book were formulated while I sat waiting for my mind to calm (most often, though, when that happens it is similar to what we experience when we awaken from a dream—the most profound thoughts fade very quickly once in deep silence. Writing a book is really not the point of meditation). Alternatively, I may have thought about a friend, spinning a story in my head about what I will say next time we meet and what it is he needs to hear from me. I may be feeling pain because of something a person close to me did or said, and I spin a tale about exactly what her motives are and how she is trying to punish me. These scenarios play out in my mind over and over until I realize I am thinking them. We are so unaware of our thoughts that we don't know we are having them.

But thoughts are just that—thoughts. We don't always cause them—they happen to us. They are necessary, of course. After all, we wouldn't get very far if we didn't plan ahead at all. At times, we need to think through priorities in our lives, and make decisions based upon those thoughts. But when we sit down in the Present, we have to realize they are simply thoughts. They come and go, like feelings, like joy and pain, like clouds floating through the atmosphere. What happens when we dwell in our thoughts, allowing what Buddhists call the monkey mind to take over, is that we limit ourselves to our stories. Many traditions speak of the Divine as Infinite. Sufism teaches that not only is the Divine limitless, but humans have an infinite spiritual vitality. Kabir Helminski writes,

"Life is infinite, and this infinity can be tapped. The only limitation is one of awareness."[12] *The Gospel of Thomas*, written by and for early followers of Jesus, suggests that the reason we have spiritual resources within us is because we are created in the image of the Divine, as suggested in Genesis as well.[13]

Yet we become limited when we get caught in the vicious cycles of stories we tell ourselves. Rather than thinking we are in the image of the Divine, we dwell on our brokenness. It is only lately that I have understood the point of meditation is not to do it right at all. This is one of the lessons of aging—letting go of our expectations, and not caring what others think. We might even get to the point where we stop torturing ourselves about whether what we think is right or not. We might even become that compassionate to ourselves. Brother Roger, the founder of the Taizé community, encourages us to be gracious to ourselves when he writes, "God is never, never at all, a tormentor of the human conscience."[14]

Teresa of Avila writes that she used to be tormented if she became distracted during prayer, until she realized she should not worry—for it is possible that the mind could be agitated while at the same time that the soul could be fully present with God. "Remember, if you want to make progress on the path and ascend to the places you have longed for, the important thing is not to think much but to love much, and so to do whatever best awakens you to love."[15] She encourages her readers to be gentle when thoughts arise, to stop analyzing the experience of mindfulness, and simply allow even a moment of stillness to occur. She writes, ". . . the soul shouldn't try to analyze the state she's in; it is a gift given to the will, not the intellect. Let the soul enjoy it without any effort beyond a few loving words."[16]

12. Helminski, *Living Presence*, 11.

13. Pagels, *Beyond Belief*; Gen 1:26.

14. Roger, *God is Love Alone*, 32.

15. Teresa of Avila, *Interior Castle*, 91.

16. Teresa of Avila, *Interior Castle*, 108.

The point is just to be. And in doing so, we get to know our-selves in some pretty interesting, and sometimes scary ways. So my mind is racing on a specific topic—I learn that I am obsessed with that. So my gut is turning with fear about something in the future that may happen—I now know how much I fear that. I have had some mystical experiences in meditation, but most of the time it is just time to stop. To stay. To be. To not have to do the dishes or type at my computer or feed the dogs or return that phone call or pay the bills (which, when I am doing those things, will be just what is happening in *that* moment), or worry about my son or feel guilty about something I said to my daughter or rush off to work.

In silence, we listen, as Jesus called followers to do. Listening can sometimes take us to places we may not want to go, however. We may be inundated with streams from our unconscious, such as emotions that are difficult to face. Father Thomas Keating suggests a spiritual director may be necessary to help us sort out psycho-logical and emotional experiences arising during silent prayer.[17] Entering the darkness, a time of profound doubt, can actually be an important part of a spiritual journey. It is a time we learn to let go of our ego. St. John of the Cross describes the "dark night of the soul" as synonymous with "contemplation."[18]

Issan Dorsey, Zen teacher and founder of Maitri Hospice for AIDS patients, writes that in the hospice environment they did not try to run from the dark places:

> We have created an environment that allows anxiety to be present. Rather than hiding from it or trying to avoid it, we actually created it as part of how to take care of the present moment. Because it *is* a part of the present moment. We will

17. Keating, *Open Mind*, 92. Keating describes the "Unloading of the Unconscious" in chapter 9.

18. John of the Cross, *Dark Night*, 58. It is important to note that the "dark night" St. John of the Cross is describing is an involuntary experience of depth beyond what most of us will experience. In Chapters 7 and 8, he discusses the "night of sense" experienced by beginners of contemplation, which may be closer to what we are describing here.

not escape the anxiety. We will not escape the fears that we have. Our function is to allow all that to be present and to settle with it, to allow ourselves to enter into that part of ourselves we are trying to avoid.[19]

A work stemming from four thousand years ago reveals this experience of darkness is as old as humanity itself, and that entering the darkness begins by listening. Inanna, Sumerian Queen of Heaven, finds herself entering the underworld with the act of listening: "From the Great Above Inanna opened her ear to the Great Below. My Lady abandoned heaven and earth to descend to the underworld." Her spiritual journey begins as she enters the underworld. The descent, beginning with opening one's ears, has impelled mystics since the beginning of human experience.[20]

Most days, we have a choice when our mind races and our emotions become strong—we can simply allow our emotion to just be there, or we can "spin out," a term used by the spiritual teacher Pema Chödrön.[21] What we tend to do is create an elaborate story surrounding our emotion that carries us into mental and emotional realms that are not reality—but are just our thinking. Chödrön advocates practicing loving kindness toward ourselves.[22] Rather than somehow thinking what we feel is wrong, we simply sit with what is. Just stay, even when your arm aches or you are hungry or your emotions are so strong you do not think you can bear them. When we stay with our emotions they will stay with us, to the point we may want to run away. But thoughts and emotions do not have power if we see them for what they are—they come and go. We just stay. It is time to just be in this moment. This is the place of Presence.

19. Schneider, *Street Zen*, 190.
20. Wolkstein and Kramer, *Inanna*, 52, 156.
21. Chödrön, *Comfortable*, 7.
22. Chödrön *Comfortable*, 9–12. See also other works by Chödrön.

A BRIEF MEDITATION

Try this. Find a quiet place to sit. Sit straight, so you are not tempted to sink back into a pillow and fall asleep. In fact, imagine as you sit in a chair with your feet planted on the floor, or cross-legged on a cushion on the floor, that there is an invisible string grounded in the earth that moves up through your tailbone, along your spine, neck and head that gently lifts the top of your head upward until you are sitting tall, straight and easily balanced.

Close your eyes. Focus your mind on your breathing—be mindful of each breath as you inhale, then exhale. Once you are focused, allow yourself to hear the sounds around you. Notice how even the hum of a computer or fluorescent light is never constant— it has variations within it. Allow the sound of a car or plane to literally move into your hearing then move out and fade. Let sounds float across your consciousness—like clouds float across the sky. They come and they go.

If you do not hear well, or if you want to continue this exercise in another way, allow your awareness to focus upon the movement within, and the feelings in your body. Mentally scan your body. You might sense your own heart beating, stronger, then more and more softly; whether your foot is falling asleep as you sit quietly; some churning in your stomach; an ache in your lower back. Let these sensations move in and out of your awareness. None of them are permanent, but fluctuate, strengthen and fade.

Then return, and gently bring your attention back to your breath. Inhale and exhale several times.

What we learn from this exercise is, first, that we are unaware of the present—much of the time we don't even realize we are breathing, or that life is going on within and around us. Second, we learn that everything comes and goes, like the sounds around us. There are no constants. Sometimes we think that the guilt we carry or the grief that settles in our heart is always and forever and will never change or lessen or leave. Of course it will—in time all things come, and all things go. What we have as a constant is simply the present—we are alive. In the Presence of Life and Being Itself.

YOUNG PEOPLE AND LIVING IN THE NOW

In some ways, persons in their teens or twenties may intuit this better than those who are older. Alicia, a college senior, helped me understand how she and her peers think. She says change happens all the time for them, and they are used to it. Things didn't used to change this quickly, she reflects. But when students in her generation hear about something new, though their first response is a startled, "Oh!" they soon follow up with, "Ok, that's cool." She gives the example of when her cousin announced he was gay. She says her reaction was typical of her peers, when she thought, "It's not for me, but it's cool for him."

Another time I was visiting with some university students when cell phones were becoming prevalent and text messaging was just beginning to catch on. One fourth-year student turned to his peer and asked, "Do you text message?" His companion replied that he did not. But, they reflected, the first-year college and high school students—their fingers were racing a mile a minute over the keys of their cell phones. Indeed, it was right about then that I looked at my family's cell phone bill and was astonished to see my teenage daughter had sent or received over twelve-hundred text messages within the previous month. Yet young people only five years older did not use this technology. Similarly, soon after, I tried to find some alumni of our program by using Facebook (which every college student used at the time, so I had my son set up an account so I could enter the on-line conversation). I discovered students only a year out of college had never heard of Facebook. Soon after this it was difficult to find a college student who didn't text, and most alums became on-line friends. With technological advances occurring so rapidly, it is possible that younger generations will grow up understanding better that nothing is constant, and that everything comes and goes.

Jesus said it best, "Listen." If we listen, we hear that sounds come and go. He also said, "Watch." We can watch, or pay attention to, the feelings of our bodies—becoming aware of feelings within that surge and disappear in time. Or we can watch the world around us. If we observe, we see that life changes. I have a tree near my deck on which I can literally witness new buds each morning in the spring—change is that quick. In the fall, the leaves fall even faster than they emerged in the spring.

In stillness we see change, also called the impermanence of life. We find a depth and richness in silence that cannot be experienced when there is noise and distraction. We come to know ourselves, and to know our connectedness with one another, in the profound stillness deep within us. Teachers of Contemplative Prayer suggest this ancient form of prayer takes us to a deep place of silence and a wide understanding of connectedness. Recall Elijah's experience as recorded in I Kings, when he was feeling alone and despondent upon learning Jezebel sought to kill him. He witnessed a great and strong wind, an earthquake, and a fire, but finally, the place he found God was in a "still, small voice."[23]

A SECOND MEDITATION

Try another exercise. While sitting straight and focusing on your breath, repeat a word with each breath. You might think of a word for Presence or Divine, such as Creator, Spirit, or Being, that is meaningful to you—preferably with two syllables so you can repeat one syllable when you inhale, and the other when you exhale. Whenever your mind begins to wander and thoughts enter, say silently to yourself "thinking," and return to repeat your word and focus on just breathing. Continue this for ten minutes, adding a minute a day until you reach twenty. After a number of days, being in Presence will become a reality of daily life.

23. I Kings 19:11–12.

Another way to begin meditation is to breathe slowly, counting "one" the first time you exhale, "two" the second time, and on, until you reach ten. If you make it to ten, start over, and count again, until your thoughts are stilled. Many discover these practices are easier with a teacher, and within a community or group.[24] As we sit in silence, eventually we do not have to chase our thoughts away, but the silence simply emerges, like the sun appearing from behind a cloud.

I once sat with a Buddhist teacher who practiced meditation for many years. He said that he still sometimes sits down to meditate and begins to count, and cannot even get to the number ten, because his mind is racing. The most important thing is never to chastise yourself because you can't get it right. Just taking time out is significant. Sitting in silence is itself enormous. And even a moment or two of stillness is more than many of us normally have in a day or week.

Being, sitting in Presence, is a gift we give ourselves. It is a way to be gentle with ourselves, whatever our emotional state is at the time. When we were children, a time out often meant punishment. I suspect most of us would give a lot to get some time out as we grow older.

And things happen. One day I was sitting feeling sad for probably the hundredth time because I could not be with one I love. I let the feelings be—not justifying them or letting the stories surrounding them take over and cause a million other emotions to swirl inside. And as I sat with the feelings, separating them from longing for the person I was missing, I realized this was bigger than my solo experience of loneliness. It was bigger than my missing him at this moment and our inability to be together. It was about learning to live with loneliness, learning to live as a human

24. The method of Centering Prayer by Thomas Keating is available in pamphlet form, as well as DVDs to assist in starting a contemplative prayer group. Events and retreats are also offered. See www.contemplativeoutreach. org. For guidance and specific meditations to practice, see also works by Brach and Chödrön.

being. It was about solidarity with all who are lonely. It was about knowing this feeling, too, will pass as new life arises.

I recall being led through meditation exercises from various faith traditions by a Sikh Guru at an international conference in Vancouver, B.C. To my untrained eye and ear, it seemed that what these practices had in common was repetition—for long after I was ready to untangle a yoga pose, cease dancing around the circle, or finish a repetitive phrase—each exercise continued.

At one point, I sat facing a partner, cross-legged, knees touching, doing a meditation that from a distance, might resemble the child's game of patty-cake. My partner was a German woman who spoke little English. To my astonishment, she never broke eye contact with me. I silently challenged myself to meet her gaze continuously (as the exercise went on and on. . .) and I soon noticed her eyes were the same hazel color as my own.

It wasn't until later that it dawned on me that I had unconsciously hit upon a fraction of wisdom our teacher meant to convey through that exercise—if we meditate long enough, we come to know we are, in some sense, one. Two women, meeting in Canada, yet living very different lives in Germany and the United States—equal and connected. In a way, we had become one for the brief duration of that exercise—for in her eyes, I saw a reflection of myself.

The *Tao Te Ching* portrays wisdom in the paradox that when one sits in silence and stops the voices of the world, one comes to understand a connection to that world:

> . . . Close the senses,
> shut the doors;
> blunt the sharpness,
> resolve the complications;
> harmonize the light,
> assimilate to the world.
> This is called mysterious sameness. . .[25]

25. *Tao Te Ching* #56, in Cleary, *Essential Tao*, 43.

4

Discovering the Self

CLOSE THE senses, shut the door, and enter into Being, or listen, sit and watch. When we live this way, things happen as we go about our day, too. It may seem depressing to let go of the notion of God the Father who has our life figured out, and a plan ahead that we just don't know about yet. It may feel as if our life is just random. However, if we are aware and awake, and attuned to the present, we will connect with others who are also aware and awake in the same healthy way. We fall in love because we are drawn together in One Spirit. We form an activist group to resist a form of injustice because we meet people with the same passion in the face of real needs around us. Things really will just seem to come together as though they were meant to be.

SYNCHRONICITY

As long as we don't understand ourselves to be puppets disciplined by some parental God figure, this understanding can be found couched in more traditional language. This may be an understanding separated only by semantics on the part of persons who talk about God in a more anthropomorphized way. My friend Sharon and I sat with a woman from an African American church located in a Midwestern city, at a conference we attended on Christian worship. Janelle said to me that when their pastor left, members of her church felt despondent and unsure. She said it was at that time that, "God woke me up early one morning and led me to scripture." There, she opened her Bible and found words of encouragement from Paul's letter to the Ephesians that have since helped to uphold her and her congregation.

Then Janelle, Sharon and I listened together to Anita tell her church's story. Her southern Hispanic church lost members when they were without a building in which to worship for several years, even worshipping in a funeral home for part of that time. The first week in their new sanctuary, a new family came and donated large gifts to the church. As we listened, Janelle jumped into the conversation, excited to point out that because Anita's congregation endured suffering and never lost their faith, God was now rewarding them and opening a new path.

I do not doubt Janelle's sincerity for a moment. She expresses, using different language than I might, that we can trust. When we endure and trust, we feel moved to act, and our lives and community begin to gel. This is not the same as expecting that when we pray for specifics, there is a God that will grant them (to those who behave correctly and have enough faith). It is faith and trust, plain and simple.

We do not control the future, as much as we may spend our time fretting about it. We could live our immediate lives with confidence and faith much more deeply. It is interesting that many of us fail to manage the events we could, but instead are desperate to control the bigger issues of our lives. Some of us, for example, are perpetually late, cramming way too many activities or meetings into one day, so we cannot really be present where we are. Most of us, most of the time, could control our daily schedule better. Instead we fret over the big stuff that we really cannot control at all—like whether or not another person loves us, or whether we will become terminally ill, or of course, when we will die.

What happens when we are living in the present, in Presence, in a spirit of realism for what is happening now, and in a spirit of compassion, is synchronicity. We talk about the importance of timing. When we live healthy lives and dwell within the present, in Presence, we come together when our realities meet in the perfect present moment. As people living in Presence, we are never really alone—we are journeying alongside others who are also awake and aware.

We all know exactly what it is to live in the moment, and to respond to the needs of others automatically. We have done it, unconsciously. As I write, my daughter's miniature dachshund is ill. While I am working around the house, I suddenly notice I am rinsing the dishes or answering the phone or even typing these words with my right hand only, as my left one is holding the little dog. I don't even realize I picked her up—she likely sidled up to me with a nudge or a soft whine and my automatic response was to lift her into my arm.

But then there are those times I am fully aware, see her come close to me, and take the time to pause as I lift her up. My life is then enriched by this small being, who nestles into my lap with a spirit of calm that is contagious, if I pay attention. Anyone who has had such a pet, or raised children, or been a caregiver of any kind likely knows that we do things in the moment for others. And we know that when we are fully present and mindful in our caregiving, we are less resentful or preoccupied or distracted.

We learn to touch deeply when we sit silently, and when we go about our lives awake and aware. We touch with our hands, aware of what is before us as if for the first time; we listen with our ears and hear anew; and we touch with our mindfulness—conscious of this very moment. When the Buddha was asked what he and his monks practice, he replied, "We sit, we walk, and we eat." When his hearer suggested that everyone does those things, the Buddha replied, "When we sit, we *know* we are sitting. When we walk, we *know* we are walking. When we eat, we *know* we are eating."[1]

Jesus calls us to sit, watch and listen. And he spends a great deal of his time eating with friends and strangers, in communion around the table. All people do those things. But we do them alongside another one of his teachings: to wake up. We do them as

1. Nhat Hanh, *Living Buddha*, 14.

awake human beings, not dwelling in the past or future, but fully present. The fruits of living in Presence are the fruits of the Holy Spirit: faith, charity and love.

BECOMING CONTEMPLATIVES

As we seek a way of contemplation, we may or may not find that we are one of those people who can become a contemplative just through practice. But we may learn to see beyond ourselves, to find both stillness within and connectedness to a greater Spirit, not by steady effort but when crisis hits. We may discover our contemplative nature through intentional practice, or it may come to us through catastrophe in our life. Many of us have had the experience of having our world wrenched apart—and being faced with a choice, to either dig in our heels and panic, or to open ourselves to new possibilities.

The notion that when we are in crisis, we are offered the possibility to wake up anew to life, is one we learn from many modern spiritual teachers. [2] And with the help of psychology, we learn that people move forward in moral and spiritual development when there is a fissure in their lives. The opportunity for growth occurs when what was supposed to be simply isn't anymore, and a new and deeper understanding of Presence is called for.

We may experience this in an abbreviated way when we travel. Phil Cousineau discusses travel as a spiritual journey. It is at the point, after we have anticipated, planned and embarked upon a journey, that we enter a labyrinth. The labyrinth has been understood for hundreds of years as a path that meanders.[3] When we walk a labyrinth, sometimes we find ourselves close to the center, other times we are surprised we are so distant from the center, at the margin. When we journey, at some point, we inevitably lose

2. Parker Palmer discusses how difficulty can be the catalyst for deepening meaning in our lives, in *Let Your Life Speak*. See also works by Chittister and Chödrön.

3. See Chapter Five, "The Labyrinth," in Cousineau, *Art of Pilgrimage*.

our way, things go wrong, and we do not know where we are. There, we are faced with a choice—to complain that things are not right (and usually blame others for that), or to realize we could not have anticipated all that this journey has to offer—and to open ourselves to the gifts that will unfold. This is wisdom that we have the opportunity to embrace when our plans go awry. When my colleagues and I travel with college students, and something goes wrong (barely catching a train by a few seconds, for example— my students will recall that harrowing experience), we have found that it is that very experience that begins the process of real group cohesion, once we catch our breath and the grumbling ceases. Opportunities to grow occur most fully when things go wrong according to our best laid plans, and our egos are threatened.

THE EGO

The paradoxical words of Jesus, that if we lose ourselves we will save ourselves, embody a truth found in much wisdom, ancient and modern. Psychologists talk about the ego, the part of ourselves that we think is all there is to us, but that really is only a small portion. Carl Jung pointed out that the ego is that part of ourselves we are conscious of, but that just below the surface is a whole world of the unconscious we have yet to explore. For Jung, redemption was possible as one discerned, through psychological processes, the hidden Self. For him, this was equivalent to the discovery of God.[4]

Because the ego isn't really our authentic self (which is called Essential Self in Sufism, or the Self by Jung), no wonder we are devastated when something happens to alter our cherished identity. We were someone's wife or husband, but that person divorces us or dies; we were an active parent, but our child grows up and moves away; we were someone's son or daughter, but our parent dies or disowns us; we were a particular kind of professional, but

4. Edinger, *Ego and Archetype*, 103–4.

we lose our job. It is as if our foundation is pulled out from under us, because the ego that identified with our role thought that role was the essence of who we were.

This wisdom that we are not just a single outward appearance comes from many places, in addition to psychology. Philosophers discuss the fragility and situatedness of identity, and how one part of our identity may be salient at one time, while another is prominent in a different context. Our identity, feminist philosophers tell us, forms and shifts within community.[5] There may be different expectations of the moral roles of males or females in some communities, for example. We can challenge and change our moral and faith understanding as at various times different parts of our identities are more important to our self-understanding. We are not fixed, and there is much more to us than meets the eye.

Siddhartha, the Buddha, taught the Four Noble Truths. The first is that all life is suffering. The second is that the cause of that suffering is desire. Thirdly, suffering can come to an end. Finally, he formulated an eightfold path to end suffering. This path enables one to develop a clearer sense of the self and reality, helping one to see that desire, the cause of suffering, is the grasping of the ego.

The ego sees the world through a distorted sense of its own importance and its separateness from all other life, apart from context and community. The ego includes our thoughts that are often fabricated stories, not based in reality. It includes the emotions we tie to the thoughts that we have fabricated about the actual events of the past or what we imagine will occur in the future. Often the ego is the identity we have developed and show to the world (and ourselves) and the way we like to be seen. The ego loves form, and is not interested in pure Presence or formlessness. In fact, the ego is not interested in what is best for us at all.[6]

5. Benhabib, *Situating the Self*, 8, describes her goal to discuss the moral self as situated within contexts of gender and community throughout the book.

6. See Maguire, *Essential Buddhism*, 86–95, for a more detailed description of the four noble truths of Buddhism, and Tolle, *A New Earth*, Chapters 2–4 for discussions on the ego.

Sufi teachings do not advocate banishing the ego, but befriending and even coming to love it, so it is no longer in control. The ego has positive qualities, such as diligence and aspiration, that are also good, when coupled with love and greater wisdom.[7]

Letting go of the ego is not letting go of ourselves. It is getting out of the way, and letting loose those things that we think are the essence of ourselves, but are not. What is real is that we are alive, we are present, we are in a particular place, born in a particular century and country, and are here now. Ideally we develop our talents and further ourselves and work and contribute to the world around us, but those talents or that job are not all of who we are by a long shot.

DISCOVERING OUR INNER VOCATION

College students are focused on what they will do when they graduate: what career, job, or vocation they will embrace (and some, on how much money those will bring). In campus ministry we deconstruct those terms. We distinguish between jobs and careers, and a vocation. Projections show that young people today will have half a dozen careers (note not just individual jobs, but actual careers) in their lifetime. Gone are the days that one went into one field and stayed there for forty years. Gone are the days when one's identity could depend upon a particular career.

But that doesn't mean people do not have particular gifts and talents. A vocation is something more akin to one's gifts, like teacher, pastor, or healer. The latter, for example, could be a healer of people—a vocation for which there are dozens of jobs and careers possible, from counseling to nursing to social work. Or healer could mean a fixer of things—such as a car mechanic or a computer technician. I recall Karen, a woman I worked for, when she was Dean of the Graduate School at my university. She was in

---

7. Helminski, *Living Presence*, 64.

an administrative position, but she always insisted she was, deep down, a teacher, no matter what job she took on.

Writers tell of the death that occurs deep within when they are not able to exercise their true vocation of writing. Women who we now know as famous writers have often discussed experiencing such muting when the demands of family and other work overwhelm their inner vocation. Tillie Olsen writes of a time when, "For a few months I was able to shield the writing with which I was so full, against the demands of jobs on which I had to be competent, through the joys and responsibilities and trials of family. For a few months. Always roused by the writing, always denied. 'I could not go to write it down. It convulsed and died in me. I will pay.'"[8]

Indeed, much is at stake when the inner self is not allowed to awaken. Creativity and transformation of both ourselves and others is thwarted. Writer Gloria Anzaldúa also writes about this experience when life gets in the way of writing. She says that for her, part of the process of writing is musing, or "awakened dreams." In them, "I am playing with my Self, I am playing with the world's soul, I am the dialogue between my Self and *el espíritu del mundo.* I change myself, I change the world."[9]

The ego encourages us to mix up the outer aspect of our career or job or family status or social status with our inner gifts. But we are not our outer work. If one job or career ends, there may be dozens of other ways to share our talents with our community and the world. Letting go means learning to cherish the present, rather than the identities or ideas we cling to. We learn to just live, not to insist or argue or judge. We learn to listen and watch.

When we focus on our work and the identity that the world sees, we ignore our inner soul, our true self, or the wisdom Jesus says is within us in the Gospel of Thomas. Parker Palmer borrows the Quaker phrase "let your life speak" to discuss the shift from determining what our life will say or be, to listening to what our life

8. Olsen, *Silences*, 20.
9. Anzaldúa, *Borderlands*, 70.

wants to do. He writes, "Before you tell your life what you intend to do with it, listen for what it intends to do with you." [10] He discusses a time when his career by all appearances was going well, but, he concedes that such appearances do not matter to the inner soul.

Many of us live lives that reflect messages of what our life "should" be. We hear from society, our family, our heritage, or others expectations, what we ought to be and we actually become that. We react, but what we don't do is really listen. We do not listen to hear what life wants to live in us. The word vocation is related in its Latin roots to the word for voice. We do not listen to our inner voice.

ENDING DUALISTIC THINKING IN FAVOR OF HOLISTIC THINKING

Breaking down dualistic thinking is a theological issue for those who have been taught that God is "out there," and that we should not trust our human longings or desires because they are sinful. We may have been taught to mistrust our own will, because only God's will is right for us. This dualistic separation between the human and the Other leads to a great deal of guilt and shame. We force ourselves to be something that is contrary to our inner selves, because we believe ourselves to be innately sinful. Mindfulness teachers show us that once we come to see what is, we discover there is no dualism between self and other, or inner and outer as we develop such awareness. [11]

I recall a small book I carried around for some time during my early years in college that still may be in use today. It had a simple drawing of a train car on each page, and explained with the first car what comes first for us as Christians, and with the last what we should pay attention to last. The simple formula was "fact, faith, feeling." The fact of Jesus' death for me was first, believ-

10. Palmer, *Let Your Life Speak*, 3.
11. See, for example, Chödrön, *Comfortable*, xiv.

ing in that fact second, and finally the insistence that we should trust our human feelings last, trailed behind on the caboose. Many Christians have been taught that our inner voice is sinful.

When some Christians hear the phrase Jesus speaks in John's gospel, "I am the way, the truth, and the life," their first conclusion is to create a dualism: Jesus is the true way (i.e. accepting Jesus as your Lord and Savior is the way) and all other ways, meaning all other spiritual paths, are by definition false.[12] But if we read Jesus' words in a non-dualistic manner, Jesus' words take on a new richness. In fact, many understand him to be referring to the "way" he acts in compassion for others (which one need not be a Christian to do) as the only "way" to salvation.

The great wisdom of the early church founders resulted in the concept of the Trinity—God as Three in One. This theological concept ideally prevents Christians from naming God by any one name, or in dualistic terms. The Trinity has reminded Christians throughout history that we cannot say God is one thing but not another. Encompassed within the Trinity are the wide-open notions of the All, the Human, and the Spirit. The problem is that the church has taken this concept and made it into doctrine—rather than recognizing God is all three of these and no one of these alone, the church has made the Trinity into a doctrine where "He" is only these (Father, Son and Holy Spirit), and nothing else. Similarly, the early church held that Jesus was both fully divine and fully human. Hence, a Christian cannot claim Jesus is one thing and not the other, such as more human than divine, or the other way around.

In the West every realm of society is steeped in dualistic thinking, and saddled with such contradiction. I was a doctoral student taking courses in American Studies when academics were infused with post-modernist thought. A basis of modernism that there are universal, overarching truths was debunked. It was deconstructed in favor of theories about dualism (where the dualisms themselves were then deconstructed).

12. John 14:6.

Postmodern thought insists that every time one names a particular thing or truth, one must also acknowledge its opposite. In fact, its very existence is dependent upon its opposite, and would not exist without the other, such as light and dark, or new and old, or truth and falsehood. Women, we learned, were defined by what they were not: i.e. men. Blacks were often defined by society as not being white. While there is, if I may be pardoned for saying so, truth in this, we can also see the problems with the dualistic thinking that dominates in the West. Groups and individuals are not allowed to self-define in a society that defines them solely in relation to another.

In addition to dualisms, we learned about hegemony, a concept that explains that societies or groups are acculturated to act unconsciously in certain ways that are often detrimental to themselves, thus continuing practices that may make no sense, or that keep the powerless in their place. [13] We came to understand how a social norm was interiorized. For example, women in our society often are the ones who teach their daughters the very values that restricted their own choices, thus reinforcing patriarchal values and limiting their daughters' opportunities. And we went on to question whether this outer/inner process in itself was a fabrication and a false dualism. [14]

Today it seems to me hegemony is at work both within us and outside, not just in one place or the other. We act in ways that restrict us personally. We allow others to define us by what we are not, rather than defining ourselves according to our own inner vocation. We become so convinced of the story or stories we have learned and absorbed about who we are and who we think we should be, that we will ourselves to become that person. And because we think dualistically, we are convinced that the "I" we

13. I am using the term hegemony more specifically than it is commonly and quite loosely used today to mean a kind of cultural consciousness.

14. See Vicki Kirby's discussion of the theory of Judith Butler, especially p. 111–12, in *Judith Butler*.

have become is right, while being anything else is wrong. We focus on whether an action or a career are considered good or bad according to society, our family or our co-workers, and we alter our behavior accordingly.

Yet, scriptures are packed with the undoing of the paradox of good and bad, exposing the falsehood of dualistic thinking. In the beatitudes, Jesus fills the heads of his hearers with paradox: "Blessed are you poor, for yours is the kingdom of God."[15] In this short phrase, he brilliantly exposes and undoes the dualistic, false mythology that the poor are poor because they have done something wrong, a belief held in Jesus' time (poverty as divine retribution) and yet in our day (poverty as the result of not trying hard enough); coupled with the notion that, therefore, the wealthy are blessed.

From cultures that are not built upon dualistic thinking, we learn the all-encompassing nature of Presence as all of Life. Spiritual wisdom the world over teaches us to overcome our dualisms. The *Tao Te Ching* says, "True sayings seem paradoxical." Also, "True words are not beautiful, beautiful words are not true. . . . Sages do not accumulate anything but give everything to others, having more the more they give."[16]

From The Four Noble Truths of Buddhism we learn that our grasping for happiness results in unhappiness. Pauline Thompson rightfully says, "I somehow doubt that one can be a Christian at all if one is unable to deal with paradoxes."[17] Jesus says the ones who lose their own life will save it. African Christian friends suggest to me that we cannot separate the sacred from the secular, especially in a world where real life issues, Christianity, and native religions coexist daily. The inadequacy of reducing life, events and the Divine to dualistic ways of thinking, is exposed not only within Eastern thought, Gnosticism and conventional Christianity, but

15. Luke 6:20.

16. *Tao Te Ching*, #78, #81, in Cleary, *Essential Tao*, 58, 60.

17. Stearns, *Writing Pauline*, 73.

most poignantly in Native American culture. Joy Harjo expresses this continuum of self and life, when she suggests that in prayer, one's whole self is opened, "To sky, to earth, to sun, to moon; To one whole voice that is you . . ."[18]

LISTENING TO OUR INNER VOICE

It may seem selfish to pay attention to our inner voice, to set aside the ego that listens to all the other voices of what others want from us, and to listen within. But my experience and wisdom from many spiritual teachers leads to the opposite conclusion. According to *The Gospel of Thomas*, Jesus teaches listeners not to pay attention to where others say the realm of God is, but that it is found only through knowing oneself:

> Jesus said, "If your leaders say to you, 'Behold, the kingdom is in the sky,' then the birds in the sky will get there before you. If they say to you, 'It is in the sea,' then the fish will get there before you.
> "Rather, the kingdom is inside you and outside you. When you know yourselves, then you will be known, and will understand that you are children of the living Father. But if you do not know yourselves, then you live in poverty, and embody poverty."[19]

When we look everywhere around us for clues and are forcing ourselves to be something we are not, for purposes of prestige, wealth, or even servanthood, we are engaged in a constant act of violence against ourselves. We live in poverty. But when we listen to our inner voice and stop feeding the ego, we become a person that others are blessed by. Of course, some people will not like it if we change. They may not have their perfect hero to worship if that is the role we played, or they may not get their service work done, if that is what we did for them. Thus, many will resist our transformation.

18. Excerpt from Joy Harjo, "Eagle Poem," in *How We Became Human*, 85.
19. *Gospel of Thomas* Saying 3, in Meyer, *Secret Teachings*, 19.

We ourselves resist the most, of course. We do not believe we are worthy of happiness, or doing what we really want. Yet when we do not fully accept ourselves we know, somewhere deep down, that something is wrong. We may feel taken advantage of, we are hurt, or we feel stuck in a relationship or job that is not life-giving for us. When this happens, we quickly interpret our situation and tell ourselves something is wrong with *me*. Tara Brach calls this the "trance of unworthiness."[20] The only way out of that trance, she says, is the cultivation of radical acceptance. We begin with ourselves, waking up to reality, and coming to accept ourselves wholly and with love.

Eckhart Tolle uses the term "pain-body" to describe emotional pain that accumulates and that we carry with us from the past. It is revived when new pain arises, and at times we even seek out situations or persons that will help revive it as our pain-body seeks attention and to be fed.[21] Our pain-body enables us to create an incredibly dramatic and self-satisfying story that magnifies our current pain, when we allow those past memories to dominate, rather than living in the present.

When we hold ourselves in compassion, our hearts begin to open up as we see others are caught in their own trances of unworthiness and fear, dominated by their pain-body. We learn by falling deeply into the Present that we are loved, and in that love we are connected with all others. This is not a process of resigning, defining ourselves according to our limitations, or self-indulgence. For when we are compassionate to ourselves we will extend that compassion to others, who are also caught in the dance or sometimes a violent tug-of-war with the ego. We will do unto others what we also do unto ourselves. Thomas Moore suggests we need to let go of the idea that the human soul is meant to be understood "successfully and properly," and of ways we thought we should live.[22]

20. Brach, *Radical Acceptance*, see chapter 1.
21. Tolle, *New Earth*, see Chapters 5 & 6.
22. Moore, *Care of the Soul*, xix.

When we live authentically, we drop our judgment of whether others are living the life they are supposed to live. We come to see perfection is not the goal, but authenticity. We learn that good and bad are always with us, and we don't always know the difference. We don't always know what another person should be, nor do we know the outcome of a particular event, whether it will be positive or not. You may know the story drawn from a Taoist perspective, "The Farmer Whose Horse Ran Away." Huston Smith tells it this way:

> On hearing of the misfortune, the farmer's neighbor arrived to commiserate, but all he got from the farmer was, *"Who knows what's good or bad?"* This proved to be true, for the next day the horse returned, bringing with it a drove of wild horses in its train. This time the neighbor arrived with congratulations, only to receive the same response. This too was so, for the next day the farmer's son tried to mount one of the wild horses and broke a leg. More commiserations from the neighbor, with the same response which was again validated, for soldiers soon came around commandeering for the army, and the son was spared because of his injury.[23]

That is not to say that when we see ourselves clearly, we have to just accept our life and resign ourselves to it. We may come to see we are living a life that is bad for us. In fact, if we are living a life that does violence to our soul, when we begin to wake up, we will see that clearly for the first time. Perhaps we are not respected, are taken advantage of at work, or even abused in our own home. That is a reality we need to see, if it is so—and likely with the help of a therapist as well as being in the moment, we need to understand that is exactly where we are right now. We can stop creating stories about why whoever abuses or takes advantage of us has every good reason to act that way to us, and see reality as it is. We can see that we are a human being who deserves love and respect as all humans do. And we can come to understand that life is about

23. Smith, *World's Religions*, 141.

change, meaning the next moment doesn't have to hold the exact same reality as this one. We can reclaim our own life.

We might also learn if we are present-focused, that we ourselves are the ones taking advantage of someone else. It may be that we hold our own principles and needs and even beliefs to be so unchanging and right that we do not see the effect we have on others lives. But the reality may be that we are demanding for ourselves at someone else's expense. And again, we can see that the next moment does not need to be the same as the present. We can change. And we will be amazed, as we read in the Gospel of Thomas:

> Jesus said, 'Let one who seeks not stop seeking until one finds.
> When one finds, one will be disturbed.
> When one is disturbed, one will be amazed,
> and will reign over all.'[24]

Disturbing or not, whatever we need to learn in the present moment will become manifest to us. It is as if we have an invisible circle around us. Everyone who steps into that circle has something to teach us. I know I have trouble with a certain personality type, and seem to find myself surrounded with just such people. As soon as one person who displays these characteristics I have trouble coping with is no longer in my life, another appears to take his or her place. It occurs to me that they may keep showing up until I learn to let them be, without my own negative reaction. Much of this is about letting go of our own control, and letting be what is. We cannot change what is at the moment; we can only watch and listen, in order to accept and determine how to move on in a healthy way in our lives.

If we hold the only truth, we become the judge of others— anyone else who thinks differently is obviously wrong, and in some theologies, so wrong as to be eternally damned. Instead of insisting, we can learn to listen, here and now. Instead of clinging to our own arguments, we might learn from the vast diversity of life surround-

24. *Gospel of Thomas*, Saying 2, in Meyer, *Secret Teachings*, 19.

ing us. Instead of claiming we know better than anyone else just who God is and what God wants, we can simply sit in Presence. When Issan Dorsey, founder of the Maitri Hospice for AIDS patients, was diagnosed with AIDS-related lymphoma, he came to define compassion as "endless dimensions of this moment."[25]

We can just listen, watch and then minister to the needs we see in our lives, and in the lives of others. We may even be more aware of pain in the world and in our own lives, and learn to face reality in a new way.

25. Schneider, *Street Zen*, 191.

5

Living With Suffering

"HE RAPED me!" After a number of conversations with me about a night she spent with a young man that continued to haunt her thoughts and feelings, a young woman (I'll call her Barb) was sitting in my office saying she finally realized she had been raped. It is not unusual for a young woman today to deny that a rape is a rape, because of the stories we as a community build up about rape that they adopt to their own situation—it is not really rape if she was willing to mess around to a point; it is not really rape if she was drinking; it is not really rape if she knew him beforehand (even though most rapes are committed by acquaintances)—these are not rape because the story is that she asked for it and brought it upon herself. But if a person just sits with the facts—she said no and he went ahead anyway—they are what they are.

Barb's suffering was caused by her experience with one man, and even more, by a culture in which this is all too commonplace, that told her stories she convinced herself were true in her own head. As she sat with me, finally having realized what really happened, she was angry. Barb insisted, "There has to be a reason! Some good has to come out of this."

I suggested to her for the time being it might be enough that her eyes were open, and that she saw that she was wronged, and that she was good, and that she deserved better. Then she came up with meaning to her experience: she realized she was not alone. For suddenly she looked at me as she remembered our conversation the night before in a discussion group, in which we were focusing on the last moments of Jesus' life. She said to me, "Jesus cried, 'why me?' too, didn't he?"

YOU WILL ALWAYS HAVE THE POOR

Jesus, we know, suffered, and if Jesus is present with us, if Jesus is Presence, we are never alone in our suffering. Pain is real. Yet, what we see in Jesus' life is that suffering does not have the last word. Death gives way to Life, especially if what we have called God is really Life and Being Itself. But we have to acknowledge the reality of suffering in ourselves and others lives in order to see this. We have to open our eyes to reality and not just the stories we tell ourselves about how the suffering is justified or unreal.

Seeing suffering in Jesus' life, and hearing his words to the disciples when they chastise him for allowing a woman to pour expensive oil upon him that could have been given to the poor, "You will always have the poor with you," make it seem like suffering is pretty entrenched in human life.[1] What are we to make of this? That poverty and the suffering accompanying it are inevitable? Some suffering can be avoided. The suffering Jesus suffered, and countless persons suffer daily—at the hands of human cruelty— that could be avoided. That could be lessened if people lived with compassionate hearts, and will be as more people learn to live in the present with compassion.

But the reality is that suffering and pain do happen, and likely always will. A young person is raped, a loved one dies or we are separated from another we love; a person undergoes chemotherapy or is injured in a car accident; a hurricane or flood devastates an entire community; a child is alone. These causes of pain are part of our world. Jesus says there will always be poor, and we can assume that means hunger and homelessness. Jesus says simply: "You will always have the poor with you, and whenever you will, you can do good to them…"

1. Mark 14:7.

I recall a question that was posed to Father Thomas Keating, when he gave a series of talks in our town. Bob, whom I know as a man of integrity and passion who would lead the way in his church and our city to rid the world of all poverty if he could, asked Father Keating what we should do about suffering in the world. I had the feeling Father Keating's response was not received as quite adequate, when he replied, in part, that there would always be suffering. When one speaks from the point of view of simply living in the present, of seeing all as Being, this is true. To surmise what the world would be like without it is simply not real—poverty and suffering just are. That doesn't mean we should not try to eliminate the causes of poverty at all. It means the human world is what it is, and that includes suffering.

I heard the same question posed to Father Keating, asked in a different venue of Brother Alois, Prior of the Taizé community. He responded that it is easy to talk about suffering in general, but in so many words, told the questioner that there is no such thing. There is only the particular suffering of specific individuals. We must not dream of a world without suffering, which does not exist, he suggested. Instead we must acknowledge the reality of suffering. Then, we see that suffering is terrible, but is also there that we find humanity. He went on to tell the story of a young boy he met who was facing a debilitating disease. We find humanity within suffering when we practice compassion, unafraid to sit with those who suffer. One way the Dali Lama defines suffering is "the feeling of unbearableness at the sight of other people's suffering."[2]

In her reading of the Gospel of Mark, Raquel St. Clair also discusses unscrutinized suffering versus the specificity of pain. Suffering is agony that is a static condition. This is neither what Jesus experiences, nor what he expects his disciples to undergo. Pain, however, is "named, recognized agony that can be trans-

2. Dalai Lama and Cutler, *Art of Happiness*, 116–17.

formed into something else." It is caused by human moral evil, and is specific and dynamic. This pain leads to transformation.[3]

LISTENING TO PAIN

As a pastor I have sat at the bedside of persons when they are dying. I never feel what they feel, nor should I. But as I enter that space, sitting close to a person with his or her hand clasped in mine, what I feel is honored. It is a place of honor to be allowed to sit with someone at such a vulnerable time, to just be there, knowing there is nothing that can be done to change death's approach.

I experience the same when a college student, like the young woman I described earlier, enters my office and, hesitant at first, slowly begins to share his or her deep pain. Sometimes I even experience being in this place of honor when I am standing in the vegetable section of the grocery store—when a person stops me and I suddenly realize what I'm hearing is not simple chit chat but deep sharing or confession. I am sure people start such conversations with me often but I don't really listen—because I am too focused on finding the freshest bunch of romaine lettuce, or in my office too preoccupied with a document that I just opened on my computer screen.

If and when we are present, however, if we sit with the pain or suffering, we know we are in a place of honor—the present—surrounded and within Presence. Sometimes just listening to a person is enough to bring about healing for them. Sometimes we are moved to act on their behalf, or to encourage them to do so. Sometimes Presence is all there is—sitting together in this moment. The thirteenth-century Sufi poet Rumi writes how pain and suffering become our teachers:

> This being human is a guest house.
> Every morning a new arrival.
> A joy, a depression, a meanness,

3. St. Clair, *Call and Consequences*, 36.

some momentary awareness comes
as an unexpected visitor.
Welcome and entertain them all!
Even if they're a crowd of sorrows …
The dark thought, the shame, the malice,
meet them at the door laughing,
and invite them in.
Be grateful for whoever comes,
because each has been sent
as a guide from beyond.[4]

We want to run from suffering, of course. And to have more pleasant and ecstatic experiences than just the mundane, let alone the painful. My friend Kristine is a respected pastor in our town, among both her own congregation and the entire community. In the past several years, she has experienced far more than her share of pain. The death of her sister, just 50 years old, leaving two school-aged daughters behind, and after living many years battling Hodgkin's disease, was devastating enough. But Kristine herself has had a recurrence of her own epilepsy, with seizures that have literally taken her months to years from which to recover.

Kristine shares with me that her mental perception is not what it used to be. Getting to a place of a mystical, spiritual vision during her meditation is actually quite easy, she says. But she sees the truer spiritual experiences when meditation is just normal, just still and silent. And when life is just grounded. She has come to learn it is not through the great mystical experiences or theological breakthroughs that we grow in faith and ministry, but by slogging through everyday life. By living through days that she is unable to focus, the days when she misses her sister, the days when the pipes break or the church gets broken into one more time, and just the plain ordinary days. In the dailiness of life, we experience the Sacred.

It is in the ordinary living of life as we listen and serve that our awareness of Presence grows, a process we are mostly unaware

4. Rumi, "The Guest House," in Barks and Moyne, *Essential Rumi*, 109.

of. Jesus compares the realm of God to a mustard seed. One does not see it growing, but it becomes a great shrub that the birds of the air use for their nests. Other parables of Jesus, also found in Mark 4, are attempts by Jesus to get his audience to listen and really hear the need to be rooted and centered, as in the parable of the sower who sows seed in unfriendly conditions only to have it dissipate, until finally he finds fertile ground. A person of faith is grounded not in the riches of this world, but in God. Jesus discusses the measure each person receives: "For to him who has will more be given; and from him who has not, even what he has will be taken away."[5] This saying, tucked between parables, indicates as we give by our presence with others we will receive more richness, but those who do not share will not also receive. These parables not only call a person to be grounded and to give, but to resistance toward the structures of society that would determine that those who are in positions of wealth or have egoistic power will receive more, and others less.[6]

Kristine's experience has deepened her ministry and ability to be present with others. She notes that we realize only after the fact that it is daily events and living with pain that strengthens us. Faith comes through resisting the seduction to do only work that is public and praised. Growth occurs when she sits with a couple grieving their daughter who died at an unfairly young age, or with another couple where one is watching the bright intellect of his partner of sixty years slip away due to dementia. Then, when she sits without answers but in pure presence, she knows real Presence.

In fact, she and others who share their journeys with me, such as Walt, a retired minister and friend, admit that as they grow older, they have less and less to say, and feel less need to preach. Walt is engaged in a ministry with Hospice, with persons who are in their last months of life. He acknowledges there is not much

5. Mark 4:25.

6. See Ched Myers discussion of this passage, in *Binding the Strong Man*, 177–9.

to say about such times, except to comment upon the ministry of "being with."

The truth is that what Walt knows and experiences in his hospice ministry, the rest of us dearly need to hear. But his ego no longer thrives upon public presence and praise. The ego fades and authenticity emerges through growing from experiences of suffering and being. I think of Moses before the burning bush—who when in the presence of his God was told to take off his shoes, for he was standing on holy ground. That is what we do in the face of deep pain.

We hear from therapists that facing our own pain—going down and through—is the best way out of it. When we face our own pain, being present and sitting in Presence with that pain helps acknowledge the pain and that it is real, and that it simply is. So often we try to run away—I know I do.

MY STORY

My son was born with a birth defect that made him unable to keep his food down. Hence, as a baby, he lived with constant gastrointestinal reflux. Of course, he could not tell us that, nor did he display any of the classic medical symptoms to alert doctors to what was wrong. All we knew was he didn't eat much, and by the time he was a year and a half old, he began to revert: having learned at one point to climb down the stairs, he went back to crawling backwards down them. He was weakening, and it took a number of specialists and quite a few tests at Children's Hospital in Milwaukee to determine what was wrong. On his second birthday, he had major surgery.

I look back on those years and wonder how we all survived. I know I did not have much awareness of my emotions, let alone the ability to simply dwell in the moment. I was the pastor of a suburban church, my husband was in his medical residency, and our son was chronically ill. Severe sleep deprivation pretty much sums it up. My husband and I sought a marriage counselor, as we found ourselves turning on one another for someone to blame. After just a few sessions, however, our counselor said he didn't think we had marital problems—just that our individual coping skills were inadequate. I then commenced a series of personal therapy sessions.

I will never forget the time I walked into the room for an hour session, and stated in fury that my husband did not react the same way I did when our son kept us up with his coughing all night. "So?" Scott, my therapist responded. I wanted to throw a lamp across the room at him.

But gradually I learned that looking to others to confirm our reaction is simply a way of holding them back from being themselves, and a way of denying our own reality. I recall an interview I conducted with Pauline Thompson when I was doing research for her biography. Early in her life, she had married a man who, according to everyone around her, was a completely unsavory character. I asked why she married him. She stated simply and profoundly that it was clearly because he was a "perfect reflection" of how she felt about herself at the time.[7]

I became convinced (and still am) that letting another go on his or her personal journey is one of the secrets of a successful partnership. And my spouse and I did, throughout the years, go on a variety of journeys, always one providing support as the other struck out—at various times one of us returning to school, or changing jobs, or going half-time at work for awhile, or changing churches or choosing not to go to go to church at all. As a family we joined in many outdoor adventures, and often went on separate journeys—as I accompanied my son (who grew up to be a healthy young man) and daughter on various wilderness flat-water canoe trips. And although occasionally I was roped into joining them, I spent a lot of my time steeped in anxiety as my husband, and at various times my son and daughter, pursued their passion for more extreme sports, including mountain climbing, black diamond or

7. Stearns, *Writing Pauline*, 32.

off-run tree skiing, and white-water canoeing and kayaking. Yet even through my fear and anxiety, I got pretty good at letting my husband go on his own journey, I thought. Until his journey took him away from me, the only other time we returned to marriage counseling.

There is a scene in the movie *The Jane Austen Book Club*, where Sylvia, played by Amy Brenneman, is sitting on her bed, weeping. Her grown daughter and her best friend are listening and comforting her. Her husband has just left her for another woman. Suddenly, her friend says, "Did he have a brain tumor?" and when she receives a negative response, retorts, "I'm rooting for the brain tumor."

The story I finally embraced about what happened to me was that it was a brain tumor that took my husband from me. I recall sitting with him in our twenty-fifth year of marriage, in our living room on a cold January evening. He had taken a leave from work and was devoid of energy. We were talking about the events to come. In ten days he was scheduled for brain surgery. He had only known about the tumor for a month, since Christmas. Yet it had been a strange autumn. I was shocked and puzzled when he had said he thought he was changing, and he contemplated leaving me. That January evening as I sat on the couch with him, I suddenly realized for the first time that I could really lose him, to death during risky surgery, or after, as he walked out my door.

I realized that fleetingly, but of course it didn't sink in. After his surgery, which was thankfully successful, I told myself in time he would recover. No, I told myself in time he would be his old self, and we would have the same loving relationship I was missing. As the months passed and I thought that things were returning to normal, I was repeatedly jolted out of my comfort zone. I experienced his reactions and actions in situations we had been in a hundred times before to be new and unpredictable. Life felt surreal. I felt unsettled, even quite often unsafe. I lived with a kind of terror inside.

In the months and years to come I would learn the stark reality of living with pain and loneliness, as he recovered from surgery but still, in time, chose to leave. His story is obviously his own, and he lives his own life today. My story is one of grieving and of learning to live with what simply is, not with what we believe things to be or what we think they should be.

My reactions in the months leading up to and following my husband's surgery were, upon reflection, driven by a combination of panic, love, and unexamined theology and family values. There is no question an important part of my identity for twenty-five years was that of being wife to a particular man, an identity that brought with it social circles and status connected to his work; being seen as a married woman with a supportive partner in my own profession; and included being a partner as a parent, having a shared history and friends, and moving toward the future together. I had much to let go of, that I once assumed was simply essential to who I was. As a friend of mine said to me, when my husband left, "We grieve the things we never even *had*—like our future together!"

Self-blame and a willingness, even desperation to change for him, and to get things back to the way I knew them before, drove me. For a long time, I clung to my belief that we were meant to be together forever—anyone who had ever known us would vouch for that. I could, by my efforts I thought, hold this together. Our family was meant to be. And I was willing to give whatever I needed to make it possible. I considered quitting my professional job to be there more for him, if that's what he needed. As a feminist the latter went against my every sensibility. But as a minister? Had I come to the place we all eventually do—the place we take up our cross and bear it? The place we have to make sacrifices in a martyred act of faith?

ACCEPTING OUR HUMANNESS

I began to re-think the Christian theology I grew up with. I cringed when a pastor urged me in a sermon to decide what cross I would take up. I'm not even sure what the preacher meant by it—but my reaction was to think, "Don't insult me ... I didn't choose this. This suffering chose me." And as I re-read other's experiences, from Job to Jesus, I realized their suffering, likewise, chose them. I began to question where we ever got the idea that they chose to suffer and that our redemption primarily comes in making the ultimate sacrifice along with Jesus. Jesus says, "If anyone would come after me, let him deny himself and take up his cross and follow me" in the midst of his predictions about future trauma in the gospel of Mark—meaning that persons who will be asked to denounce Jesus should instead participate as his followers.[8] I wondered anew why we view God as a sadist who demands suffering for salvation in our time. I came to wonder what possessed me to think sacrifice of who we are, completely changing ourselves (not just care-giving, as many of us do with an ill loved one; but become a completely different person) is something our God requires.

I was broken, for sure. And I did a lot of things a parent is not supposed to do, including lean on my teenage daughter. A year later, she reflected upon her experience of her father's tumor and her parents' divorce. She revealed her perception of those months, when she wrote about her mother: "It was a kind of role reversal for a while, where I became her parent, and she became someone I had to take care of, 24/7."

It was my daughter, actually, who helped me learn to let go as she and I developed a new relationship of trust. Through our relationship, I began to understand what it means to accept reality as it is, rather than to live in a world I fabricate in my own mind. She was clearly going to make her own decisions, and helped me to realize one choice I had as a parent was either to give into the temptation to

8. Mark 8:34.

close my eyes, or to take the opportunity to listen. I grew to respect her, as we communicated about the reality of what went on in her teenage life, as opposed to what I wished would go on. But all that took time. Eight months after my divorce, although I knew the divorce had to happen, I was still deeply grieving the man I loved. I was exhausted. It was the end of the school year, and my tired body was reminding me that my professional work responsibilities, being a single mother, homeowner (oh, could I go on!) was more than I had ever had to bear alone before. I travelled to Taizé, France with a group of college students and pastoral colleagues.

Many of us have a place to which we return that is sacred to us. For me, the Taizé community in France is such a place. I have taken college students on pilgrimages to the community several times, and most recently returned with my daughter. At Taizé, the community and hundreds of guests sit together in prayers three times a day. On this particular week-long visit, I sat in the Taizé church long after formal prayers were finished more than once, and wept. "I can't do this alone anymore," I thought. And finally, one afternoon in the silence of the empty church, I heard: "What do you mean, alone?" Of course that would be the answer. I am in the midst of Presence every minute of my life. I believe I heard that answer because we tap into wisdom that is far more accessible than we might think, from deep within and from the Presence surrounding us, if we listen.

HOLDING OURSELVES IN COMPASSION

I returned to Taizé a year later. Again, I hit bottom. I was feeling undeserving. Like I didn't even deserve love. Not only had my marriage crumbled, but by this time I had met another man I loved, but who I was unable to be with. I felt like Sylvia again, in that scene in *The Jane Austen Book Club*, as she wails to her daughter and friend. "My body will become a museum!" It's amazing the scenarios we create.

I was sitting at Taizé feeling about as sorry for myself as you can get. When I described the scene later, my friend Carolea noted that my pain-body was at its best. Indeed, being in this trance dominated by my pain-body enabled me to completely erase the fact that I have an incredibly supportive family, and friends who have been true gifts, unfailingly present with me throughout recent years. Not only did I feel lonely, forgetting all these blessings, but I told myself I should be ashamed to even be at Taizé. I shouldn't even take up space here, I convinced myself—don't the brothers really want young people to come here? Isn't that what this place is for?

I then had a chance to talk with one of the brothers (guiltily, of course, feeling I had no right to take up his time). He was French, and spoke a little English. He listened. He told me Brother Roger (the founder of Taizé) used to say there is a special place in us only Christ fills. But then he looked directly at me and asked, "But how long were you married? ... Yes, this is hard." We sat in silence, and I spoke a few words, but mostly just wept. Finally, I said, "I don't feel like I deserve to be loved." He suddenly sat up straight, his eyes brightened, and said to me with his French accent, "But it is not *possible!*"

Even Jesus, after the resurrection, the brother reminded me, asked Peter, "Do you love me?" It is not possible that a human does not deserve love. It is human to ask for it—even the one who was supposed to be beyond human needs, the *resurrected* Jesus, asked for it.

Of course the brother was right. Trying to be inhuman, above human, thinking we can do without love is another form of thinking we are better than everyone else. We see in Jesus that love is crucial—loving your neighbor *as yourself* he said, is the second greatest commandment. How often we confuse humility with not loving or taking care of ourselves, allowing our own minds or others' words or actions to put us down. Sitting in the present, and sometimes getting help from a spiritual teacher or counselor, enable us to see that we are simply human, and to seek in healthy ways the respect and love we deserve.

Sister Lillian, from the Monastery of St. Gertrude's, served as a spiritual director for me throughout the initial years I was losing hold of and grieving my marriage. I probably didn't meet with her enough, and at times was so self-absorbed I couldn't hear her. What I do recall, though, is that she just sat through the trauma with me. And that at the end of each session together, she gave me a hug, and said, "You are good!" "You are good!" as if to add, "And don't you ever forget it!" We rarely hold ourselves with such compassion.

My experience, although deeply painful, may not actually be unique at all. When I felt the most sorry for myself, I thought about Job, who lost everything, and who questioned God. And I realized the question really is not "Why me?" The question is "Why not me?" We all suffer. When I visit elderly persons in my community every one of them teaches me this. Every one of us will face disaster, abandonment, illness, wounds, and if we don't suffer a lot before then, finally we will when we face the loss of our life as death approaches.

The first two noble truths of Buddhism teach about the suffering of life, and how we create our own suffering by our thoughts. I certainly brought a lot of suffering upon myself. One of the most fascinating things about being hurt is the stories we spin in our own minds explaining why someone is intentionally inflicting pain upon us. When my husband threatened to leave me, I was sure it was because he misunderstood me and just didn't see the depth of my love. I was sure his leaving was due to delusions of a better world elsewhere, when I knew we could make it a better world right here.

I see now that things could not have been other than they are. As Byron Katie says, "If you want reality to be different than it is, you might as well try to teach a cat to bark."[9] I see now my

9. Katie, *Loving What Is*, 2.

husband had undergone profound changes, and had to leave. And I do believe a person needs to do what she or he has to do to follow their journey. (I believe that, of course, unless it takes someone away from me!) But for years I spun stories about what he must be thinking and what I thought just had to be. Of course, I could not know what he really thought, and worked myself into all kinds of emotional states over my created version of reality—which were not the present reality at all.

It is inevitable that each of us will experience suffering, and we all have our opportunities to ask "Why me?" or "Why not me?" Suffering is real, yet much of it is fabricated by our constant justifications as to why we were wronged or why we were misunderstood or why this is someone else's fault or why we ourselves should be punished. The pain itself, though, just is what it is, and most likely will not change with the stories we tell (more likely, it will grow worse). As time progresses, we may even be able to recognize loneliness or sadness and say, "Here you are again, accompanying me today," as though suffering is a companion beside us. We might, as Rumi suggests, welcome loneliness into our home as a teacher. Naming and recognizing our sadness lessens its power.

Much suffering is brought on by ourselves. Much suffering, though, is brought by one human being or community upon another, and hence could be avoided. The trial and pain on the cross suffered by Jesus, for example.

6

Understanding Jesus' Suffering

JESUS DID not die for our sins. Jesus died as a result of human sin. Jesus came to bring us a new way to live—a way of radical acceptance of one another, of living deeply in the present and in the Presence of the Divine. He came to bring a way of inner peace for us, and to bring what he called the realm of God on earth where peace reigns.

Humans missed the point (or rather got the point just fine and found it threatening) while he was alive—and killed him. We miss the point by couching all his teachings in doctrine and dogma and theologies of exclusive salvation, and the way he taught remains dead to us today.

Already by the third chapter of Mark and early in Jesus' ministry, we see that the authorities are planning to trap Jesus. They try throughout the gospel, by asking questions that he brilliantly turns on their heads. Each time, what they object to is either his popularity with the crowds, or his willingness to set aside religious dogma. When he heals a man's withered hand on the Sabbath, going against religious teaching, his opponents immediately counsel with one another about how to destroy him.[1] People listen to this man more than they do the authorities, and this man listens to people—showing that Presence and healing are more important than any rules or regulations. This is truly threatening to the powers that be.

---

1. Mark 3:6.

THE PASSION OF JESUS

The passion of Jesus has often been understood to be totally about Jesus' sacrifice given as atonement for human sin (sometimes called substitutionary atonement theology). The movie *The Passion of the Christ* depicts events of Jesus' arrest and death on the cross in this way. Its debut was a formative event for many of us in campus ministry, and to this day the movie frames the majority of our discussions and discoveries about those last days of Jesus and what they really meant.

The film was set to come out on Ash Wednesday. The movie itself was so heavily advertised among the media and some churches, that the local press began calling me even before it debuted in local theaters to ask my opinion of the film. Knowing those calls would be even more frequent once the movie was showing, I didn't wait until I could gather a group of students to go, but went alone to a matinee one afternoon. Almost as fascinating as the movie was the anticipation of those who were there to see it. As I stood in line for popcorn and a bottle of water, I overheard a young college student in front of me say to his companion that he was kind of scared to see this graphic and violently bloody representation of Jesus' death, because he wasn't sure he could take knowing Jesus did *all that* just for *him*.

I heard similar theology from Daniel, a graduate student who came to a weekly discussion I led. He said he was told by his former campus pastor that when Jesus was hanging on that cross, he was thinking about him—about Daniel himself—this particular individual who would live in the United States of America two thousand years later.

The Passion focuses on the sacrifice of Jesus and the insistence of the crowd that he be killed, culminating in the lengthy (a dozen minutes, although it seems like thirty) scourging of Jesus until there is no flesh left on his back. Ironically, this scene is taken from one line in Mark's gospel that is almost a parenthesis between

Pilate's deciding what to do to satisfy the crowd, releasing Barabbas, "and having scourged Jesus," delivers Jesus to be crucified.[2] The gospel of Matthew also briefly mentions the scourging, and all four gospel writers emphasize that Jesus was mocked for thinking he was a king far more than they focus on his receiving a beating. The message movie viewers receive from the film is clear, however: this man suffered greater violence, flogging and pain than any other human being in the history of the world, all as a sacrificial act for me.

ATONEMENT THEOLOGY

This is atonement theology at its most graphic. Before looking at its effect on our view of the world, it is important to realize that it is not the only way Christians have understood the meaning of Jesus' death and resurrection.

Atonement theology did not become the dominant under-standing of Jesus' death on the cross until a thousand years after his death. Recent study of early Christian sources reveals that some of the early accounts about Jesus do not dwell at all on his passion and death, but on life in Jesus. These are written in the tradition of wisdom literature and are made up of Jesus' own words (the Gospel of Thomas) or his egalitarianism and service (Q, a reconstructed source used by later gospels, especially Matthew and Luke). The focus of these early works is not on the individual at all, but on a collective, communal view of life for Jesus' followers.[3]

Many scholars note that it was not until the fourth century when St. Augustine stressed the basic sinfulness of each human being, and the need for a major act of redemption. In the late eleventh-century, St. Anselm outlined substitutionary atonement for the church: human disobedience or sin is a crime against God,

2. Mark 15:15.

3. Crossan, *Birth of Christianity*, 502–3, and throughout Parts VI through VIII.

which requires punishment in order for it to be forgiven. Jesus, the only human to live a life of true justice and sinlessness, and therefore the only one eligible, pays the price. This theology reasons that because the sacrifice had to be made and because God is merciful, God took it upon himself to offer his son as a sacrifice. At best, the cross is understood as a tool of reconciliation, where humanity is, essentially, kidnapped by evil, and a ransom is necessary for healing.[4] In the sixteenth-century the Council of Trent passed several decrees on original sin, hence establishing the requirement for an act of sacrificial atonement for sin. This doctrine became central to the church thereafter.[5]

This understanding stretches what the New Testament says, where a variety of reasons for Jesus' death are given. There is only one reference in Mark to Jesus giving his life as a ransom. This term occurs in the same breath with service: "The Son of Humanity came not to be served but to serve, and to give his life as a ransom for many." [6] Ransom has to do with serving others, offering freedom and liberation. We have witnessed how Jesus' whole life was about liberation from oppression, self-obsession and human cruelty.

Rita Nakashima Brock and Rebecca Ann Parker demonstrate through a detailed analysis of early Christian art, history and writings, that throughout its first thousand years, images of Jesus' death and accompanying theology focus on the resurrected Jesus. Paintings depict him as a living being within a society akin to paradise. It is not until after this that images of a crucified Jesus appear. The subtitle of *Saving Paradise*, this ambitious work, sums up what happened: *How Christianity Traded Love of This World for Crucifixion and Empire.*

The understanding that Jesus' primary purpose is to be crucified, rather than to usher in a world of peace and paradise on

---

4. See Michael A. Lindvall's discussion of substitionary atonement, in *Geography of God*, 33–37.

5. Fox, *Original Blessing*, 49.

6. Mark 10:45.

earth, is destructive to our life together. There are serious problems with atonement theology in its most graphic form, such as its portrayal in *The Passion*, which holds Jesus suffered the worst pain in the history of humankind just for me. Primarily is the fact that thousands and millions have suffered pain equally as horrible. We cannot assume Jesus' scourging was worse than atrocities human beings experienced in Nazi concentration camps, or worse pain than the sexual humiliation, ridicule of their religion and water boarding prisoners endured for more than seven years in a row at Guantanamo, or worse than the regular beatings suffered by a battered woman in her own home year after year. Or that Jesus' dying on the cross was more painful than the deaths of innocent persons in Darfur, or the deaths of the hundreds of thousands unjustly killed throughout the world, killings occurring even as I write and as you read these words. To say that Jesus suffered the worst pain of any human being in history is an affront to all who suffer.

That Jesus' death was all about me and my salvation as an individual suggests we are Christians just because we personally get something out of it. The claim that Jesus' death and resurrection are simply, finally, and fundamentally only about me and my eternal salvation is an insult to Christians who care about the world. Black theologians speak of sin as corporate, not individual. If we are to be free from sin, everyone has to be free, not just one individual. And many are not free because of the oppressive structures of society. James Cone equates God's salvation with human liberation in the face of oppression.[7] This means that the heart of the gospel is the activity of God throughout history, of liberating the oppressed humans from bondage in this life.

It seems to me Jesus' message is the opposite of declaring individual salvation apart from societal justice. A claim to such liberation goes against his admonition to the disciples, when they are arguing about who will be with him in heaven and Jesus insists that the first will be last, and the last will be first. Over and over he

7. Cone, *Risks of Faith*, 32–33.

discusses the importance of selfless love to those who will listen. Jesus calls for humility on the part of individuals, and addressing the care and justice of all persons corporately instead.

Another problem with atonement theology is seen in that, throughout the past thousand years, one of the horrific effects of the belief in this theology has been the justification of violence. Sometimes violence is necessary, Christianity has argued throughout the centuries, in order for God's purging to take place. This logic has reigned from historical justifications for medieval Christian Holy Wars to today when wives and children are disciplined by the head of the household "for their own good," in some Christian sects.

The book *Proverbs of Ashes* enfolds two moving tales of women emerging from abuse from the authors' own lives, intertwined with a theology of redemption. Brock reasons that in Christianity, Jesus accepts violence because he is playing the perfectly obedient son. So any salvation received through this is gained through the violence of an abusive Father, or of society that condones such violence. Like the abused child, Jesus' acceptance of violence is done out of his love for the abuser.[8] Abusive pain should never be the basis, nor the inevitable outcome of love.

Womanist theologians work from the experience of African American women, who have throughout U.S. history been surrogates and substitutes in the lives of white women, and servants for all of society. To connect this kind of act with salvation is to make invisible the suffering of these women. Delores Williams writes: "redemption of humans can have nothing to do with any kind of surrogate or substitute role Jesus was reputed to have played in a bloody act that supposedly gained victory over sin and/or evil."[9]

Questioning whether Jesus died for individual sins calls into question, for some, the entire truth of Christianity. To question this theology is to make moot the question often cited as a litmus

8. Brock and Parker, *Proverbs of Ashes*, especially 154–8.
9. Williams, *Sisters in the Wilderness*, 165.

test for Christians: "How do you know that you are saved?" It takes the focus off of me and my life, to see us as part of a human community not seeking salvation for ourselves, but compassion for all.

A central question of the Reformation from Catholicism to Protestantism, that continues to be debated today, is whether Christians are saved through human works or through faith. I view contemporary theology that focuses on salvation as a theology of works. It insists that we need to do something, including accepting Jesus as Savior and appropriately speaking such a proclamation, in order to be saved.

In our reading of Mark's gospel, Jesus died for his initiation of a revolution that would bring about a new realm of God's compassion on earth. All that needs to be done to bring about this new salvation has already been done. God's realm is here, and we live in it now. Our task is not to save ourselves, but to participate in a new way within this realm. It is time for us to open our eyes and see that we already live enveloped in the Presence and the realm of God.

Jesus calls us to community and to resistance to injustice, not to individual salvation apart from freedom for the oppressed. It is not enough, for some, that Jesus lived and called people to a new way and a new world. It is not enough that those who suffer for justice' sake further the reign of God and work of Jesus on earth. It is not even enough that we can now be in communion with the living Christ. Instead, for many, it is essential to know that we have it right, we have our salvation sewn up, that we know exactly what God requires.

Yet questioning atonement theology does not mean we are neither forgiven nor unable to move beyond bondage to the selfishness in our nature. There are many ways we can understand the biblical definition of forgiveness apart from the need for horrific sacrifice. Many scholars have demonstrated that the understanding of a sacrificial lamb in the Bible (which Jesus was and is compared to) has nothing to do with suffering or substitution, for in Hebrew tradition sacrificial animals were killed quickly and efficiently. The focus was never on the suffering of the animal. Neither was the animal's life seen as a substitution for a human who otherwise deserved to die for their sins.[10]

Forgiveness does not require the sacrifice of Jesus. Consider this: if sins are only forgiven through Jesus' death on the cross, John must have been deluded as he called people to repentance for the forgiveness of sins. Yet, Jesus seemed to trust in him, and he himself was baptized by John. Consider also how Jesus' own ministry is filled with pronouncing sins forgiven, before his death on the cross has taken place. The reason Jesus' habit of going around forgiving sins is so controversial for the religious leaders of his day is because it bypasses the need for a temple sacrifice in order for sins to be forgiven. Jesus' actions engender their anger. He himself becomes angry at the hypocrisy of religious people and overturns the tables of the moneychangers in the temple.[11] That particular action, flying in the face of authorities, is often regarded as the last straw and the reason Jesus was arrested.

Most of the time, Jesus pronounces sins forgiven even before any confession is given by the sinner. Jesus demonstrates the unconditional nature of forgiveness, not even requiring confession— again a radical departure from the need to go to the temple and participate in ritual in order to be eligible for grace. Through countless proclamations of forgiveness in the gospel of Mark, Jesus himself overturns the need for a sacrifice or even specific words of repentance, in order for sins to be forgiven.

If the Divine is Presence, and we live fully in the present, we must look hard at present reality and seeing ourselves for who we are. This is the beginning of profound forgiveness. Forgiveness is part of healing in the living of our lives. To imagine a God who

10. Borg and Crossan, *Last Week*, 37–38.
11. Mark 11:15.

requires violence and blood to make that happen is simply not necessary.

WHY DID JESUS REALLY DIE?

We have gotten our theology backwards—it is not that Jesus suffered for us. Jesus suffered because the world was not able to understand him. Jesus came to bring about a different kind of reign on earth—where compassion rules, where people are healed and fed and taken care of by community; a world where religious rulers do not take advantage of the poor and political rulers do not lord unjustly over people. A world where justice and egalitarian distribution throughout society is the norm—where the lines between rich and poor are not growing more divisive, but where compassion rules. A world that contrasts with one where the dominant power that allies itself with religion rules.

Jesus begins the last week of his life with a radical, carefully-planned non-violent counterprocession demonstration through his entrance to Jerusalem. In *The Last Week*, Marcus Borg and John Dominic Crossan describe the last seven days of Jesus' life as portrayed in Mark's gospel. On Palm Sunday, the Roman governor, Pontius Pilate, heads into Jerusalem with a regal procession of horses as a proclamation of imperial power. On the same day, across town, Jesus enters Jerusalem on a colt walking over a carpet of leafy fronds laid down by the common people, announcing the power and reign of God.[12]

Jesus' entrance into the city is also reminiscent of a Jewish Messianic prophecy, according to Adela Yarbro Collins. He is called the coming one, and associated with the Davidic Messiah.[13] Where Jesus differs from the expected Davidic Messiah, however, is that the former was anticipated to come as a political, military

---

12. See "Palm Sunday," in Borg and Crossan, *Last Week*, 3, and all of Chapter 1.

13. Collins, *Mark*, 71–72.

ruler. Jesus the Messiah is one who will suffer and die for the life he has lived, a life that has threatened the authorities. He ushers in not a new political rule, but the just rule of God.

The Roman ruler is known as the Son of God, which means he is the representative of God and bringer of peace on earth. Note the first time in Mark that Jesus is called Son of God (other than by unclean spirits possessing a person) is at his crucifixion by an imperial centurion, who may know perfectly well he is contrasting the Roman empire with this humble leader.[14] He is going so far as to verbally unseat the empire in favor of this humble peasant. This Jesus, as representative of God, brings peace and compassion to all, rather than being compassionate only to those the government finds convenient, while punishing others with violence.

Jesus dies because his vision of the world is so threatening to the ruling powers they cannot let it be. He mesmerizes the crowds, outwits the scholars who ask questions to try and trick him into blasphemy, and embodies by his actions a deep message of Judaism, his own religion—that people are meant to live in a society humbled in the Presence of Divine, not human power, where all are treated with kindness. This is threatening to any in power, and is bound to get him killed.

Jesus prophesies his own death, outlining what will occur in some detail to his disciples in Mark. Jesus knows from the first year of his ministry that there is a plot to kill him—the authorities are constantly seeking ways to trap him. Many insist he believes it to be something God requires for the salvation of future Christians, although he never says that himself. It is more likely that he knows he will be killed because human beings simply do not tolerate the kind of vision, healing, community and world he demonstrates—one that pays no attention to authority but is radically compassionate.

In fact Jesus is quite detailed when he tells his disciples what will happen in those last days and hours of his life. He seems to be

14. Mark 15:39.

trying to get them to understand, and to go with him through this humiliation and suffering. He never suggests he is doing this all *for* them, nor does he say their role will be just to sit by and observe. Rather he invites them to come along and stay with him through the suffering that is coming. Note that in the end, he apparently does not succeed, because the twelve are not recorded as being near the cross.

As we have seen, the people who stick with Jesus as he requests, according to Mark's gospel, are the women: Mary Magdalene, Mary the mother of James and Joses, and Salome, as well as a number of other women who have followed him to Jerusalem. Presumably these women have either listened and understand Jesus' invitation to participate in his suffering all the way through with him, or in some organic way they grasp the importance of community and family itself—that compassion means standing by in the midst of suffering. It is not until after Jesus' death and they have stood with him through his suffering, that the women find the open tomb and flee, because they are afraid.

Because we still don't fully comprehend why Jesus came, and what kind of world he envisions—a world of compassion with—we continue to see his suffering for us as the primary reason. Hence, we continue to see suffering itself as salvific, as an act that saves us, thus celebrating the endurance of unjustly inflicted suffering. This glorification of suffering becomes an oddly and disturbingly frequent justification for causing and enduring pain and abuse. We have turned the message of Jesus into a comfortable message about me and my salvation and feel sorry that some others may have to endure pain and abuse—which they need, because they need to strengthen their faith if they too want to be saved. We have withdrawn to clusters of comfortable pews while labeling anti-patriotic any who suggest, like Jesus does in his time of his government, that our government is abusing its power and neglecting its poor.

In the Gospel of Mark, Jesus says there is only one unforgivable sin: blasphemy against the Holy Spirit. He makes this remark, we are told, because others accuse him of having an unclean spirit. His accusers are incensed because he heals on the wrong day (the Sabbath), or heals such large numbers of people, or because he can forgive sins and cast out demons. His accusers try to say he is of the devil because he demonstrates power apart from theirs, which threatens their authority.[15] Many suggest the unforgiveable sin is one of not recognizing the Spirit in Jesus, particularly as he exorcised demons. It is quite possible there was a continuing controversy in Mark's day regarding exorcisms done by Jesus or his followers.[16] I would venture Jesus' remark may also be suggesting that the singular unforgiveable sin is a failure to recognize the Holy Spirit wherever there is a true spirit of compassion.

Our world is still threatened by compassion when those in power perceive it as undermining their authority. Jesus is still being crucified, over and over. There is an interesting argument between scholars who see the cross as a symbol of power over the oppressed, and those who see a symbol of freedom from oppression for a community. Some argue the cross is an important symbol for many Christians who do experience oppression and even crucifixion in the fight for justice. James Cone insists the cross, for African Americans, is the same as the lynching tree—indeed, the cross *is* the lynching tree. When African Americans see the cross they know that Jesus experienced the same terror in standing for justice that Blacks have in our country. Those who suffer know they are not alone, as Christ hangs on that tree with them.

Some argue with Cone that the symbol of the cross is also a symbol co-opted by the oppressor. The cross is a reminder that whenever one suffers at the hands of power, every choice to suffer is also a choice to allow another to choose to perpetuate violence.[17]

15. See Mark 3:20–30.

16. Collins, *Mark*, 235.

17. Conversations and question session following "Saving Paradise: How Christianity Traded Love of This World for Crucifixion and Empire" (paper presented at American Academy of Religion Annual Meeting, November 3, 2008).

OPEN YOUR EYES TOWARD LIVING MORE DEEPLY IN THE PRESENT

But not all individuals choose—many are victims of injustice as a community attempts to gain justice for the oppressed—and the cross is a symbol of the struggle for justice for a people. Gutiérrez' experience in Latin America shows martyrdom is a consequence of resisting oppression. He writes, "Martyrdom is something that happens but is not sought."[18] We can agree the cross is not simply a cozy comfort for me as an individual, bought because Jesus allowed himself to be abused for my sake, but is about communal struggle for freedom from oppression.

Rachel St. Clair notes that each time a person, including Jesus, experiences pain in Mark's gospel, it is never a result of God's intention, but always of human action. She insists Jesus' "suffering and death are the results of moral evil, that is, the sinful reaction of human beings. And Jesus' resurrection is God's divine counteraction."[19] It is the work of social groups that causes agony for many, and Jesus' ministry is about the alleviation of such pain.

A central problem with the Christian message as it is preached today is that it focuses on the individual, not on societal injustice which is what Jesus was resisting, a resistance that got him killed on the cross. Contemporary Christian theology focuses so narrowly on the exclusive message that Jesus died for us to save our sins, that we escape our call to further the reign of God on earth, which includes justice for all people. Just as Mark portrays Jesus as a new kind of Messiah who suffers and dies, he ends with the proclamation that the story does not end in tragedy. The tomb holding Jesus' body is empty. Jesus' death becomes an opportunity for resurrection, and the defeat of death. This defeat means the community continues to experience the presence of Christ as it lives in a new realm that defies hunger, poverty and death. Because we still don't comprehend why Jesus came—to rid the world of the

18. Gutiérrez, *We Drink from Our Own Wells*, 117.

19. St. Clair, *Call and Consequences*, 124, 138. See also Chapter 2 for an excellent survey of how various scholars of the Gospel of Mark treat the relationship between ministry and agony.

structures of oppression—people who stand for justice continue to be trapped by the authorities, and many who innocently suffer go unnoticed by us. I was fortunate to meet just such a remarkable man when he came to our university.

CHAPLAIN JAMES YEE

Chaplain James Yee was the first Muslim to become a chaplain in the United States Army. A U.S. citizen of Asian descent, Yee converted to Islam after many years of study, influenced by kind and faithful people he met while on duty in the Middle East. Yee's first assignment as a chaplain was to serve in Guantanamo Bay, a place where the vast majority of the prisoners were Muslims. Yee spoke to them in Arabic, spending long hours each day listening to the prisoners, and faithfully carrying out his duty as an army chaplain to make sure all U.S. prisoners have the right to practice their religion.

Gradually, he began to realize many of the prisoners were not guilty, but were in the wrong place at the wrong time, and captured as suspected terrorists. He also began to hear from the prisoners about disturbing interrogation methods utilized to get information from them. Still, Yee never held the personal agenda of going against the army—he simply wanted the prisoners to be treated fairly while they were held by the U.S. military.

When granted a leave to return to return to the mainland, Yee was captured and detained as he landed in Florida. He was treated much the way the Guantanamo prisoners had been—blind-folded and taken to a cell without rights or representation, shackled, humiliated, and held in solitary confinement. Accusations of treason against him were spread to many, including his own family.

Yee made the comment when he was signing my copy of his book, *For God and Country*, that many persons have told him they read it right through in one sitting. I couldn't. I kept having to stop because when I read the descriptions of the inhumanity my own government inflicted upon him and upon men at Guantanamo, and the disregard for human dignity, I wept. Their, and his, religion was used as a weapon against them. Yee calls Islam the secret weapon held by the Army to use against the inmates, as, for example, the guards routinely desecrated individual prisoner's copies of their Holy book, The Qur'an.[20] It seems Christian Americans have also been guilty of misusing Islam for terrorist purposes.

It appears the Army did not trust Yee because he could speak to these prisoners as human beings, in their own language, as a Muslim himself. Some began to entertain the paranoia that he must be a collaborator with them. Yee was arrested after spending long hours listening to prisoners who had been cast outside national boundaries, and for advocating such simple religious rights as allowing them to withdraw for daily prayers. The simple act of listening to the prisoners is still, in this day and age, way too politically dangerous to the authorities.

We are still capturing and abusing persons who stand for the people. While Chaplain Yee was on his way to withdraw for deeply needed rest, he was arrested. We still don't understand, and we allow the arrests of those who work for justice to continue. When Yee was finally freed and allowed to leave the military with an honorable discharge, he did not receive an apology or an explanation of under what authority he was detained without due process.

Each of us can name persons that stood for justice who were captured, if not crucified, from our reading of newspapers or from history lessons in school. We could all name persons who work for justice, distributive justice, and what the world did and continues to do to them. Further, many innocent persons are accused because fairness and justice are far from the norm in our world.

20. See Chapter 7, "Gitmo's Secret Weapon," in Yee, *For God and Country.*

VHONDA'S STORY

I met Vhonda after learning she had been arrested for alleged shoplifting, and would face a court hearing and a jail sentence soon. She had stepped into a vestibule between two sets of exit doors to answer her phone in a Macy's Department Store in a neighboring town. When she came back into the store to return a piece of merchandise she had in her hand, she was accused of shoplifting by a store security guard.

When I heard Vhonda's story, there was no doubt in my mind she did not intend to shoplift. A freshman at the university, this young African American woman was raised by a single mother determined to see her succeed in college. She took on a double major, and planned to go on to law school. She finished high school early, and was one of those students with the drive and personality that told a person she will do exactly what she plans, if not far more.

In order to get out of the store after being held for some hours, Vhonda was told she had to sign a statement, which she did and after which, to her surprise, the police were called and she was arrested. When she appeared in court the first time, the 18-year-old was advised by her lawyer in the small, white community that she had no chance unless she pled guilty, and so she did. By the time I met her, she was to see the judge one more time and a jail sentence was inevitable, even though by then she knew she had been mistaken to enter a false guilty plea.

In court, Vhonda, the only African American in the courtroom (other than her mother, who sat watching) received forty-eight hours in jail, a requirement that she send the judge a letter every month attesting to her good behavior throughout her fifteen month probation (with a $10 bill in each envelope), and a serious reprimand. This was after I witnessed the judge suspend sentences for each white person who came before him. These included suspending four days jail time for a man who admitted he had assaulted "his woman" because she wasn't feeding the baby right;

giving only eight months probation (no jail time) and requiring a DUI (Driving Under the Influence) course for a woman whose car hit a woman with children in her car head-on, and excusing jail time for two more DUI's.

The next morning, I entered the jail bearing my clergy identification card, and was allowed in through the locked gates. Vhonda had just spent her first night in jail. Steel doors slammed behind her as she approached me in a bright orange jumpsuit. I gave her a long hug. We sat on the hard, cold chairs and she looked at me with clear, wide eyes, and a dazzling smile.

"They were so good to me last night," she began, excitedly. The jailers, she said, had asked what she was doing there, knowing she did not look as if she belonged in jail. She and the other inmates sat up and watched television and talked all night, she reported. When one complained about her upbringing and her parents, Vhonda could relate. She told me how she counseled the women not to be victims, to go back to school, and to take control. She said that she knew God was with her.

I was stilled and silenced as I listened. I felt I was in the presence of Jesus—angry, but not bitter; realistic, but able to put herself aside for others. To be honest, I felt like a fool—she was the minister, not me.

We continue to put people behind bars because we still don't understand. We don't yet get that the reason Jesus came was to bring fairness, justice, an end to this kind of discrimination that divides people and victimizes so many. We don't yet get that Jesus was killed trying to bring about a world where this will not happen.

THIS LIFE VS. THE AFTERLIFE

Suffering is a part of human life. Yet, some of it would not be necessary, were it not for the fact that we as humans hate, fear, abuse and ignore others' needs. Because we don't understand why Jesus came, unnecessary pain, abuse, war, killing, and poverty reign on this earth, and we sit by while prophets who speak against it keep getting crucified over and over, as do the victims of that injustice. We could provide all the children in our country, let alone other countries, enough food to flourish, if we cared. We could listen to prophetic voices calling us to compassion, rather than ignore or even assassinate them because we cannot bear to give up our lifestyle and convictions.

If we continue to miss this crucial reason Jesus was killed, even a small portion of the human race cannot ever come to know the healing and salvation in their lives—the new kind of justice in which Divine, not human power pervades—that Jesus envisioned. Our salvation as Christians and members of the human race on this earth depends on embracing a new understanding of what that reign of God on earth would look like.

This theology is not opposed to understanding the Risen Christ as a Presence we meet or merge with in the afterlife, after we die. But too often a focus on the afterlife and belief that all will be well in the next life becomes an excuse to neglect or even participate in the causes of suffering and injustice in this world. When a person has societal privilege or lives a relatively materially comfortable life, as many of us in the United States do in comparison with our neighbors around the world, thinking about heaven is very different than the way a person experiencing oppression might view it. We tend to think about heaven in very individualistic terms—as a place I will go if I am righteous.

As people of privilege, we need to be excessively careful not to use the afterlife as a means of hope for others who do not enjoy the privileges of life we do. We need to focus first upon ushering in the way of Jesus that would eliminate many of the conditions leading to their hopelessness. One of our greatest sins has been the corporate sin of condoning wars and avoiding peacemaking, hence allowing the conditions for, if not directly causing, such dire poverty that robs persons of hope. Turning to community and toward justice moves humans to rid of the causes of tragedies in our own country, such as hunger and the inaccessibility of basic healthcare, that our society has resisted addressing for so long.[21]

Gutiérrez writes, "Hope in the resurrection is in no sense an evasion of concrete history." He goes on to emphasize, "Belief in the resurrection is incompatible with the acceptance of a society that condemns the poor to death."[22] Rather than thinking about heaven as an escape from this life, it is inextricably linked with the struggle against the injustices that bring death to many.

Our salvation will not come through belief in any doctrine—indeed our inner salvation, and our salvation as a human species on earth, may very well depend upon letting go of human dogma and really listening to Jesus of Nazareth. The way of salvation Jesus offers presents an ancient, abiding path that can yet bring deep peace within our souls and reconciliation within our world.

It may feel unsettling not to embrace a specific dogma that guarantees our salvation in the afterlife. Those who live with pain or with terminal illness can find significant comfort knowing after death they will be in the Presence of Love. The peace and hope offered by such faith is worth honoring. Living in Presence and Love need not be limited, however, to the afterlife, nor to a select group of believers. Living in Presence and in Love's embrace is a vision we find in the compassionate way of Jesus, available to all, here and now.

21. See Emilie Townes, *Breaking the Fine Rain of Death*, for an excellent demonstration of a theology and methodology that champions care as a way out of dire healthcare crisis among the African American community in the U.S.

22. Gutiérrez, *We Drink from Our Own Wells*, 118.

7

Living in Compassionate Community

WHAT WOULD happen if those of us who are Christians stopped spreading the gospel? If we suspended our need to spread the gospel in the sense of telling about Jesus and belief in him; and simply did what Jesus called his followers to do: listen, sit, and watch? What if we declared a moratorium among Christians on talking about salvation in Jesus, or insisting on any particular doctrine, for a year, or a month, or even a day? What if instead people lived in the present moment, responding to the immediate needs within their communities, in deep Presence? Is it possible the world would look far more Christian than it does today? And that in our own personal lives we would be more attuned to what is, rather than focusing on who we think we are supposed to be?

For persons who are not in the church, taking clues from Jesus and living in Presence almost might be easier than for those who are not. If we are not part of the church community, we are not bound by its formulas and by rituals dictated by dogma. Yet we then face another problem, if we are out on our own and not part of some kind of community. It is difficult to live in Presence all by ourselves in a world that is future and past-focused all the time, time-driven and alien to notions of the holiness of time and Being. All of us have a need to learn to live in community as people in the present.

Looking at the life of Jesus, four things stand out in how he lives with others, creating community wherever he goes. First, as we have seen, his personal life is centered in prayer. Second, he talks about forgiveness. He tells people their sins are forgiven, which often seems like blasphemy to those around him, and he seems to have faith in people that they can change.

Third, he does not judge. He does not come with an absolute moral framework, lecturing about how he will not heal them because they are too sinful and unrepentant. He does not say he will not sit at the table with certain people because they have a spurious past and he is ashamed. He is open to all people, exactly where they are.

And finally, he is compassionate and loving to all—the righteous and the unrighteous alike. He heals, feeds, and forgives all, creating a new kind of order where compassion reigns on earth. Indeed, notice how much of his ministry involves food—either he is feeding the crowds, or he withdraws to a household of his close friends and they share a meal together. This is a ministry of the table—where all are welcome.

Spending time around the table seems to be the central focus of Jesus' personal life in community. Numerous times he withdraws to the homes of friends, including Simon and Andrew. There, the friends eat together and find nourishment with one another.[1] We are not isolated individuals, and we need one another. Sharing with our friends is absolutely crucial to live lives of faith and health. I know, in addition to time in meditation and Presence (which I have learned and practiced with friends and teachers), the support and unconditional acceptance of my family and friends is what has gotten me through some difficult years. Too often we let our egos think we can do it alone, but even Jesus does not attempt that.

FORGIVENESS

Jesus spends time in community, and he often talks about forgiveness. If we set aside the belief that Jesus died to forgive my sins, we can dispense with the notion that there is one giant experience of forgiveness that happens when I accept what Jesus did for me.

---

1. Mark 1:29–31.

The idea that I am forgiven and therefore righteous and saved, sets the forgiven apart as more righteous than others. But we are all human beings on the same level. We are all capable of sinning and all deserving of forgiveness. We experience forgiveness as we live in Presence and community, rather than wrapping ourselves (and thus thinking ourselves better than those outside the wrap) in Jesus' once and for all forgiveness. If we knew it was our job to do the forgiving for one another and for ourselves, we would live in community differently.

We do, hopefully, grow in wisdom as we grow older. We understand that we are forged through struggle. We learn from our mistakes. We are never perfect. Judging who is the most righteous is a judgment we might not find relevant, if we became more interested in serving and forgiving others than in securing our personal salvation.

SEX AND MORALITY

Christianity today is questioned for both its elite exclusivism, and for its individualistic bent. These are radically challenged by a spirituality that does not separate the Christian life from solidarity with those who are victims of injustice in this world.[2] Yet our church, local, and national politics, and communities focus on *individual* morality. It's true that we need to respect one another and follow civil laws in order to enjoy peace in our community and nation. Some say if we just followed the basic Ten Commandments all would be well. Interestingly, when persons insist upon judging others according to those commandments by, say, putting up a list of them on a courthouse wall, when questioned, very few of those proponents can name all ten (how many of us can?). Yet, our society insists a person is either a sinner, having broken one of these rules, or a saint. Admittedly, as local evening news programs remind us, some individuals do commit heinous sins, and

2. Gutiérrez, *We Drink from Our Own Wells*, 13–16.

our hearts are sick when we hear of families and children brutally murdered. It is nonsensical and beyond our comprehension. Some acts of cruelty are simply evil.

One reason many are fleeing away from Christianity toward alternative pathways is that people who are not hardened criminals, but ordinary human beings, experience judgment. There are some people we do not allow to come to the table in the church, or to become members, or to even be considered for the ministry. We have rules about who is eligible to be a leader, who is eligible to be a member, who is eligible to take communion. The church takes its dogmas and doctrines so seriously, more seriously than opening our eyes to people's needs around us, and offering healing where it is needed.

People both within and outside the church in the West today define sin very individually. As Christians, the sins we focus upon most acutely are usually on the part of individuals who have transgressed some doctrine we hold to be unbreakable. And we have some favorite sins on which we spend the most time.

Sex, for example. Western Christianity is particularly focused upon sexual sins. Jesus barely mentions them (when he does his words are generally ignored—as when he labels it adultery to marry after one divorces one's spouse).[3] St. Paul was worried about sexual behavior, but no more than he cautioned against dozens of other transgressions in the churches he wrote to. St. Augustine left us with more to consider regarding the sinfulness of sexuality. He viewed the sexual act resulting in conception as sinful. He grappled with the question of whether there was ever a time he could have been innocent, "if I was conceived in iniquity" and "my mother nourished me within the womb in sins."[4] Subsequently in the church, the notion of original sin became mixed up with ideas

3. Mark 10:2–12.
4. Augustine, *Confessions*, 50.

about sexuality as sinful. Yet, this notion of being born into original sin is not found in Jewish tradition, the tradition of Jesus.[5]

This unhealthy relationship with sexuality reigns in the
church today, exacerbated by a society that is confused about sex.
Our society supports an enormous pornography industry, coupled
with the continuation of Puritan sexual taboos. Many theorists in
gender studies and social sciences today, as well as spiritual teachers, note that the U.S. is a society obsessed with sex, as this paradox
demonstrates. Many recognize that we allow sexuality to have an
enormous power over us while at the same time calling it sinful.[6]

While traveling in Europe some years ago, I spoke with a
number of people about the U.S. government. They simply did not
understand our deep obsession over the Clinton-Lewinsky scan-
dal. One woman said to me, "We *expect* that our President will
have affairs—it comes with having that kind of power."

Power does breed the notion that one can get away with anything. Jesus' temptation in the wilderness is all about the seduction
of power—he can have anything he wants if he makes a deal with
the devil. The gospel of Mark doesn't go into details, but we learn
that Jesus is tempted early on, before he really begins his ministry. Hence, Mark acknowledges at the very beginning of Jesus'
ministry that this lust for power is enormous. Ironically, today as
Christians, and as Americans, we hold onto the notion that our
politicians, and dare I say our pastors, are above the human temptation of power. With pastors, anyway, we may be setting them up.
We create doctrines that have rigid moral expectations, then we
put our pastors in positions of authority and power (not to men-
tion, for some, with inadequate pay and exhausting workloads).
We then hold them to our rigid standards, and cannot understand
when they break them.

This is not to say taking advantage of a power relationship is
neutral or ever justified. It is to say we as a community are culpable

5. Fox, *Original Blessing*, 47–56.
6. For example, see Helminski, *Living Presence*, 49.

in creating the venue for individual sin to foster. We are living in our fantasy lands, not reality. When given too much power and too much stress, people do take advantage of others. And people fall in love when the circumstances and timing are completely unsupportive. People get involved.

NON-JUDGMENT AND COMPASSION

If we shift our focus from judgment to compassion, we will learn to value love and sex for the blessings they are. We begin to understand it is not exclusively marriage that guarantees acceptable sexual behavior, for coercive sex occurs even there. Instead, we begin to think in terms of "authentic consent" and the doing of no harm, as discussed by Marie Fortune.[7] Goddess religion teaches us that sexuality can be seen as a mirror, an exchange of energy between two adults. That exchange of power can indeed become distorted, as power-over in a culture of estrangement such as ours.[8]

If we focus less on insisting everyone live the life they "should" than on facing reality, we encourage authenticity by acknowledging the pain that people experience whenever things are not as we wish they would be. Our hearts open to those who struggle with the difference between what they wish was and what is, as when relationships are broken by the infidelity of one partner. We are able to simply be with persons in their suffering, a first step toward healing and wholeness.

If, however, we are operating out of rules and not within the reality of Presence, notice what occurs even when no one in particular gets hurt by an unfaithful lover. Once we label behavior as sexual, individual, and sinful, we feel particularly incensed and spend a great deal of the church and society's time, energy, and money. Take homosexual relationships. Many same sex couples are deeply in love and have been faithful to one another for de-

7. Fortune, *Love Does No Harm*, 86.
8. Starhawk, *Dreaming the Dark*, 136–7.

cades. Yet, since we define homosexuality as having to do with sex, and a sinful kind of sex, we do not open our eyes to the love, faithfulness, and integrity we see before us. Hence, the church spends hours, days, weeks, even years of church meetings debating whether a man or woman who declares him or herself gay is worthy of ordination, if not simply membership. If we were not so focused on individual (especially sexual) sin, think of the needs of people around us we might notice, and care for.

If we take living in the present seriously, we will see the world not through our doctrines of judgment of individual sin, but with compassion. We might begin to question where the larger immorality is within our communities. When we take the life of Jesus seriously, compassion for those who suffer has to be the first thing on our radar screen, whether it is persons who are ill or hungry or in pain. Jesus calls his followers to first and foremost resist oppressive government structures, and to demonstrate a completely new model of compassion and fairness. As Americans we tend to think that immorality and sin are far worse if they involve individual behavior, than with the fact that we are cataclysmically killing the earth or whole generations of young people by the regimes and wars we support.

Bill Wassmuth, Director of the Northwest Coalition Against Malicious Harassment, was a priest in Coeur d'Alene, Idaho, at a time when his community was threatened by a vicious form of hate from the nearby presence of the Aryan Nations. Wassmuth helped to lead efforts against hate in his community. He wrote:

> I think the faith community needs to establish the moral plan of the community, help frame the moral parameters of the community, and I do not mean moral in the sense of sexual behavior, but moral in the sense of how we treat our neighbor and how we interact with each other.
> I think faith communities exist to be a leaven in the larger community.[9]

9. Vogt, *Common Courage*, 70.

Wassmuth saw the possibility that people of faith can be that leaven, and can make a difference. He understood suffering, life and death make the most sense, saying as he lived with Lou Gehrig's disease near the end of his life, when one comes to see the "human spirit as being capable of limitlessness."[10]

CORPORATE VS. INDIVIDUAL SIN
IN LIBERATION THEOLOGIES

Wassmuth worked as a priest in the tradition of Liberation Theology. Emerging in the latter half of the twentieth-century, Latin American liberation theologians taught that people participate in sin in ways that have effects on thousands, if not millions of lives. They drew connections between our political alliances with tyrannical governments, and the suppression and resultant poverty of countless individuals in those countries. They took the Bible to the poor who understood immediately that Jesus was on the side of the poor, not the rulers whose wealth was made at the expense of the poor.

The gospel came alive in places such as Solentiname in Nicaragua up to and during the 1970s. Ernesto Cardenál records the discussions of Bible studies he held there. He describes how the campesinos discussed the scriptures as they gathered around the table together. After sharing a lunch of steamed fish wrapped in banana leaves and breadfruit they brought and prepared for one another, they focused on the parable of the seed from Mark 4:26-29. Their response to the story saying the kingdom of God will grow as a seed, included the recognition that, "When equality reigns among people, that will be the kingdom of God." And, "one day a society without selfishness will come into existence, as all revolutionaries who fight for it know even though they are

10. Vogt, *Common Courage*, 216.

not Christians. And we Christians know it too if we believe in the gospel."[11]

Liberation in this understanding is no less than "the saving action of God in history," according to Gustavo Gutiérrez. He describes the inextricable link between a Christian spirituality of humility that is faithful to the Spirit of Christ, and the integration of salvation with liberation for the poor. This concern for the poor is an essential element of spirituality.[12] Liberation theology mirrors for us the fact that immorality is found when we have nationally supported totalitarian regimes that kill innocent persons.

Black liberation theologians and preachers have for decades pointed out the connections between the oppressive acts throughout U.S. history and the biblical injunction to work for justice and liberation. They further demonstrate the corporate nature of sin. James Cone writes that "*black* theology contends that the content of Christian theology is *liberation*." He emphasizes, "The equation of God's salvation with human liberation is found throughout biblical history, and particularly in God's incarnate appearance in Jesus Christ."[13] He follows this connection through the black experience in America. This theology undergirded the civil rights movement in the U.S. Non-violent resistance is not just a technique, but emerges from a Christian understanding of Jesus as leading a non-violent resistance movement in his day.

African American theologians and pastors continue to remind us today that although it is masked in different ways, America is still a deeply divided nation racially. There also exists an attitude of colonization and privilege from which we treat many throughout the world. Immorality is found when we discriminate against individuals because we perceive the racial category we put them in as inferior.

11. Cardenál, *Gospel in Solentiname*, 172, 178.

12. Gutiérrez, *We Drink from Our Own Wells*, 2, 103. See also throughout Chapter 6.

13. Cone, *Risks of Faith*, 32–33.

Following on the heels of liberation theologians, feminist theologians made the connection that the "personal is political," noting that individual sins and how we treat one another impacts the lives of countless others. They stressed that within societies where there is a power imbalance, the brunt of pain is often borne by the women. The dualisms of mind/body, masculine/feminine, and human technology/earth have informed Christian theology in negative ways. A new understanding of sin, not as "pride" as Christianity had previously championed, but as lack of pride, or underdevelopment of self for most women, was posited.[14] They illustrated that gender inequalities within societies needed to be addressed if all persons are to be able to become fully the persons they are meant to be. Immorality is found when we allow some to live with abuse and humiliation just because of unequal standards between the sexes, and we look the other way.

By the end of the twentieth century, Womanist theologians astutely noted that feminist theologians were operating under assumptions that ignore factors of race and class, addressing issues that only affected middle to upper-class white women.[15] The use of the term servanthood for Christians by feminist theologians, for example, ignored the negative experience of servitude experienced by African American women.[16] Womanist theologians stressed that in the African American community, one cannot just save the women, but must work for justice on behalf of the entire community together. Mujerista and Asian American theologians highlighted issues of poverty, arbitrary borders, immigration, and discrimination that affect men, women and children together. All of these theologians, including feminist, have evolved sophisti-

14. Saiving, "Human Situation" 37.

15. See St. Clair's discussion of the adoption of the term Womanist (including its original definition written by Alice Walker) by African American women engaged in theology, in *Call and Consequences*, 12–17.

16. See Grant, "Sin of Servanthood," 208–209.

cated critiques of oppression based upon gender, race, class, sexual orientation, and disabilities.

Immorality is found when we discriminate against persons based upon race, ethnicity, gender, and social class. Without thinking (or sometimes perfectly aware of what we are doing), we assume one person is better than another because they *look* the part, or we just *think* they aren't right for a part.

Today not only Queer theologians, but a growing number of persons in the church and society understand that discrimination we participate in against gay, lesbian, bisexual or transgendered people is simply that: discrimination. Carter Heyward and others have been urging us for some time to consider the dignity of all persons, gay or straight.[17] It can be called the latest civil rights front. Like the struggle for racial equality, society will slide back many times before we finally realize our discrimination of human beings who are contributing members of society is unjust and simply wrong. Christians should be leading the way for society in any cause of justice. Immorality is found when we discriminate based upon arbitrary categories.

Finally, eco-feminist and eco-theologians demonstrate that human destruction of and estrangement from the earth is one more sign that we misunderstand that the cross of Jesus is about resistance to suffering and oppression. Creatures are dying at an alarming rate. Calling for environmental and social justice together, in an ethic of compassion and solidarity, Larry Rasmussen discusses Christian theology that promotes an ethic wherein we hear "the cry of the people and the cry of the earth together."[18] Our rape of the earth is immoral—yet we rarely think about sinning when we do something as simple as filling our car with gas. But our lifestyle of consumption and enormous lust for oil create

---

17. See, for example, Heyward, *Saving Jesus*.

18. Rasmussen, *Earth Community*, 291. For excellent examples of eco-feminist and ecological theology from this same era, see the work of Rosemary Radford Ruether and Sallie McFague.

the conditions for catastrophic accidents in off-shore drilling. As a result, we find ourselves sitting by helplessly when billions upon billions of gallons of oil pour into the ocean, choking life in the sea and ruining the livelihoods of those whose work depends upon that sea.

All these theologies teach us that our focus on individual sin is far too narrow and incredibly naïve. My student Barb's experience illuminates how our society blames the individual for rape, while constantly conveying messages to young men through media, upbringing, and custom that they are entitled to sex. We convey to rape victims it is because something is wrong with them. We focus on the individual sin of the perpetrator and the sin of unworthiness on the part of females and males who are victims of rape, while missing the fact that as a society we are culpable, as we live in a culture that fosters the attitudes that contribute to those daily acts of violence.

Every time we turn on the news or read the paper we see this pattern emerge. Many people deride a woman's choice to have an abortion as an individual sin, calling for the right to life of individuals for the nine months before birth. Yet, once born, the child is not guaranteed a right to life for the next eighteen years, as our society allows hundreds of thousands of children to grow up without adequate access to nutrition and healthcare. When we focus on individual sin our collective sin rarely appears before our eyes; it remains out of sight, out of mind.

"Open your eyes," Jesus said. As my friend Heidi suggested in a sermon to her congregation, as long as we are part of a large community that embraces power over things, and power over others in the world—to dictate terms of commerce, to exploit food supplies, to make deals with dictators, to initiate war, to experiment with vaccines on sick people in Africa, to choose personal comfort and corporate greed over preservation of natural resources—then we all take the devil's bargain that Jesus refused during those forty days in the wilderness.

COALITION-BUILDING

It is not just religious people but also secular sources that understand what we lack is humility. We are living in a culture that has developed an enormous ego. Journalists, cultural critics, and common citizens wondered how our banking industry grew to a point that it lost sight of the rightness of its mortgage practices, leading to a huge financial crisis. Many have questioned our participation in the conflict in Iraq and Afghanistan, questioning why our culture is not more discomforted by involvement in war at all, let alone the aftermath of war these countries are left with.

There are countless organizations dedicated to the elimination of discrimination based upon religion, race, class, gender, able-bodiedness, or sexuality. Many make the connections between these human stratifications and the fate of our planet. *Roots and Shoots* is just one example. Sponsored by the Jane Goodall Institute, this environmental organization is highly attractive to students on college campuses today. Goodall's work highlights the human centered egoism including racism, bigotry and fanaticism that has led to near extinction of many animal species, and continues to block efforts toward global peace.[19] Her work to save the chimpanzees is a lesson in compassion and hope, as she has come to recognize the importance of self-sustainability on the part of the human communities surrounding chimpanzee habitats. Students in this movement are making small changes in their local communities that add up to a tremendous environmental effort.

Denominational efforts to serve those in crisis are effective ways people connect with one another to fill basic human needs. Students associated with our campus ministry have worked through such agencies as Presbyterian Disaster Assistance and the United Methodist Committee on Relief, to join in Hurricane Katrina relief efforts for some years. The students do help others, and alongside the hundreds of others who volunteer a week at a time, make a

19. Goodall and Berman, *Reason for Hope*, 133.

difference. I am impressed with the learning that takes place in the students themselves. They do help others—but are deeply inspired by the courage and faith of the homeowners of devastated homes they meet. We must be careful not to engage in short-term mission trips for our own satisfaction and desire to be saviors, however. Creating larger partnerships between communities for on-going assistance is also taking place effectively by many organizations.[20] We learn it is the work of all of us as community to bring about relief, not that some of us condescend do the work for others.

If within our communities we learned to treat one another with forgiveness and non-judgment, the world would be a different place. If we listened, really listened, to one another's confessions and pain, and offered to go on the journey of forgiveness and healing together, we would hear specific things we could do something about. If we confessed that we ourselves participate in immorality together that reaches vaster and wider than the individual sins most people commit, we would open our eyes to those corporate sins and begin to change. If, radically, every person was welcome at our table, and we listened, repented, forgave, and hence transformed our lives in community, at the same time collectively examining our corporate sins, ours would be a different society. If we really understood the connection between our behavior as human beings and he plight of the earth, we would insure life for future generations on this planet.

AMY AND THE CHURCH

Many religious groups and church congregations listen, watch, and respond to present needs in their communities, although a very tiny portion of their budget and members are usually involved. We have the choice to open our eyes, to look around us and make the needs of the hungry and the poor the priority where we put the bulk of our dollars and our energy. What an amazing thing—to

20. See Mark Radecke's discussion, "Misguided Missions."

act as a community of forgiven people who know we are not the judges of one another. Imagine what would happen if we learned from Jesus: be humble, serve whoever is before you, and open your eyes. Listen. Watch. Sit.

Amy, one of the pastors of a church in my town, told me such a story. She has a heart for helping to end poverty, but since coming to our college town didn't know how to engage in such a ministry—in fact, on the surface, she hadn't yet even seen people in poverty in this community. She soon met several parishioners with the same passion, and together, they went to a local Saturday morning food bank to see what they could do. There, she discovered why she couldn't see the poor in our area—they are largely invisible. Many of the people needing help from the local food bank are students—often graduate students who come from overseas, live on graduate stipends that fall below the poverty level, and barely have enough to feed themselves or their families.

Amy discovered a whole subculture she had not known existed, even though she had previously "seen" these same people all over town. Further, her parishioners learned many were going home from the food bank without the lentils donated by local farmers, because they did not know how to prepare them. Church members began to make up pots of lentil soup and offer samples and recipes to weekly visitors of the food bank. Additionally, I know many church members who have quietly been involved in serving the community long before this, without asking for anything in return—whether the conversion of another, or acclamation for oneself.

There are thousands of examples of churches involved in such service. Methodist and Presbyterian Churches in Marion, Iowa, have been involved in hundreds of hours of assisting flood relief years after the Cedar Rapids floods. They run a thriving clothing bank for people in their town. And on top of that, they realize many young people in their own community are left alone without adequate lunches during the summer. They make thousands of lunches and deliver them to children in their own home town, with the help of other churches, daily. Parishioners and friends of a United Church of Christ in Tell City, Indiana gather each Thursday evening and prepare meals for people in their community and surrounding area who would not have adequate meals otherwise.

This service not only receives too small a portion of our budgets and attention in most churches, the vast majority of us has yet to address the causes of poverty. The church is called to address the deeper issues, such as identifying and eradicating the conditions that have fostered this enormous lack of adequate food among our nation's families. We cannot work to fight injustice for long without looking at its causes and seeking solutions.[21]

PAUL AND THE CHURCHES

I met Paul when I was invited to his community to discuss with local religious leaders how they might work together in campus ministry, as a new university was planned in their California town. Paul is an evangelist who wholeheartedly believes in the gospel of Jesus Christ, and once worked as a music minister in a large Southern Baptist church. As he drove me to the airport after our consultation, I admitted to him I was pretty floored when some members of the clergy told me flat out that once the university is up and running, they will refuse to work on campus with anyone that does not believe exactly as they do (including many Christians, as well as people of other faiths). Paul lamented that they live with their eyes closed. Then he told me his story.

In his late fifties, having raised five children and worked his entire life in the church, he had a kind of a conversion experience. He quit the church and began a nonprofit organization to assist the community. He envisioned programs for the homeless, and after-school programs for kids. He was particularly proud of the Father's

---

21. Gutiérrez makes this point clearly in *We Drink from Our Own Wells*, 107.

Program, designed to help poor, divorced fathers stay involved in the lives of their children.

Paul tried at first to get a coalition of churches together to support this crucial work. But he discovered it was not the church people that turned out to be willing to help at all. It was the unchurched. That broke Paul's heart. As we drove down the freeway, Paul began pounding on the steering wheel of his car. "We have to be Matthew 25 Christians!" he exclaimed, as his car nearly swerved into the next lane. "We have to be Christians that make Jesus' beatitudes of caring for the poor and hungry first in our lives. Those pastors of churches that would not help are too busy trying to fill their pews," he lamented. Paul said that he finally came to understand we are called to trust and to serve people faithfully, rather than solely try and convert people to our doctrine and belief. Then, we will find compassionate people of all persuasions and beliefs working alongside us to bring compassion into this world.

This work often involves interfaith cooperation. As Christians we are called to move beyond tolerance to pluralism that engages in hospitality with those different from ourselves. Martin Marty calls this the "risk of hospitality."[22]

RITUAL IN WORSHIP

Recently a woman said to me she no longer goes to worship, because there is too much noise there. Think about our worship. Some of us sing hymns and praise songs, we pray out loud, we read confessions and watch power-point presentations, we hear preacher's words, scripture readings and moving compositions from the praise band or the choir, we stand up and sit down and maybe even kneel.

This is not to say there is something essentially wrong with the varieties of worship we practice. Many people have experiences of truly being in the present when they are carried up by music, for

22. Marty, *When Faiths Collide*, 124.

example. I have witnessed persons singing together to the beat of a drum and electric guitar, swaying with hands in the air, truly in the moment and experiencing love within community. I have watched congregations sitting quietly listening to an organ cantata, deeply and peacefully resting in the moment.

Ritual helps to bring us into the Presence of the sacred. Father Keating discusses the story of the woman touching the hem of Jesus' garment, where power goes out of him to heal her, as pointing to the meaning of ritual. Metaphorically, rituals are the "clothing of God," filled with God's healing power. He calls rituals, "symbols, gestures, places and things that have a sacred meaning."[23]

Ritual can also reenact a sacred act toward bringing one into the absolute present, the presence of the Divine. Communion, in the Christian tradition, is meaningful not just because Jesus said we should eat the bread and drink the cup or celebrate his broken body and spilled blood weekly or monthly in worship, but because when the words of institution are spoken, the Presence of Christ is real. The community sits together around the table in Presence. A Seder supper in a Jewish household is not just a remembrance, but a reenactment, bringing the family members into one space with those who were a part of the Hebrew community throughout the centuries, back to the time of the Exodus itself.

I once was invited to participate in a dhikr service. As the Sufi teacher leading the service began to chant in deep, resonant tones, he invited us to join, and we grasped hands and moved in a circle. The Arabic chants were soft, then reached a crescendo. Soon, the vibrations took me to a place reminiscent of an ancient, deep time and space. Listening, watching, participating, a Presence far greater and deeper within me was awakened.

Muslims who have made The Hajj, a pilgrimage to Mecca, thus fulfilling one of the Five Pillars of Islam, describe it as a life-changing experience of mystery, awe, and connectedness. As soon as each one of millions of pilgrims arrives in Mecca, they exchange

23. Keating, *The Mystery of Christ*, 3.

their clothing for simple white dress, symbolizing the equality and connection of all the people, regardless of country of origin or economic status. During the pilgrimage, they walk particular pathways to retrace the steps of their ancestors, reenacting the walk of the faithful.

From Goddess traditions we learn that ritual can serve to both connect participants, and draw upon the inner voice within each. The community first waits in silence for inspiration. The resulting ritual evokes the inner self of the individual and the corporate Deep Self of the community. This power-from-within can also be called Goddess, Spirit or immanence.[24]

LISTENING IN WORSHIP

Even if we participate in ritual within worship, there is something missing in our community life. We rarely listen—not just to previously prepared words or songs, but just listen. We don't just sit and watch. Likewise, outside of worship or church community, and for those who don't engage in formal worship at all, we rarely just listen, just watch, just sit.

There are examples of worship involving listening and silence from the Quaker tradition, as well as in the daily prayers of monastic communities. The campus ministry I work in has been deeply influenced by the prayers, consisting of readings, music and silence, developed by the Brothers of Taizé. What consistently strikes me, as we introduce students either through pilgrimages to Taizé itself, or through our worship together, is their reaction to this worship style. When I ask them what they like best, they often say they like the music. Then they inevitably add, "But I *love* the silence."

None of us has time for silence—particularly college students, who as far as I can tell are permanently wired—to computer, phone, and music devices, including new advances I can't keep up with. But it is in silence and in community where we discover a

24. Starhawk, *Dreaming the Dark*, 157–8, 4.

new kind of peace within Presence. Ann, a young woman who went to Taizé with us, writes that she went on the trip, "expecting to have some incredible spiritual experience. I was searching for something that I could feel and find meaning in. I didn't get what I expected. I found a stillness that I didn't know I could reach. I found a sense of peace within myself."

We can create opportunities to cultivate listening in our community life. In my town a group of students, pastors and lay people recently envisioned a new kind of service we called *Mosaic* that is open to all people—inclusive and welcoming to persons of various gender, sexual orientation, and religious identities. We created a service inclusive of Christians and those who have been burned by the Christian church, as well as those who simply find the church does not speak to them. The response has been slowly growing and deeply profound. Participants sing and sit together, listening in silence and Presence as a community of persons on the margins of traditional religion.[25]

Another group of people were moved by a presentation on Centering Prayer by Father Keating, after we invited him to give a symposium in our town. Lutherans, Episcopalians and others, they have continued to meet weekly in a local Episcopal Church for contemplative prayer for years since. Another group of Christian ministers, Tibetan Buddhists, and community members sit together a half hour each week for silent meditation.

Like many such groups across the country, an interfaith dialogue group made up of leaders from the Baha'i, Muslim, Jewish, Catholic, Protestant, Latter-day Saints, and Hindu tradi-

---

25. My United Methodist colleague Robert first introduced me and our students to Taizé many years ago, and we never looked back. Most recently, the Synod of Alaska-Northwest of the Presbyterian Church (U.S.A.) awarded us a grant for one year to develop a weekly Taizé service for students in our community. The creation of *Mosaic* was made possible by a Worship Renewal Grant from the Calvin Institute of Christian Worship, funded by the Lilly Endowment, Inc. These grants offered a depth of experience for many in our ministry that is hard to measure.

tions, meets monthly in our community to learn from one another about our various traditions. Periodically (whenever we can find a good excuse!) we gather our communities together for potlucks. Sharing a meal, a central part of the ministry of Jesus and many other spiritual teachers, is a powerful point of connection. What we find is that because we meet to share bread together, when national crises occur that may affect one or another of our memberships most acutely, we are able to come together immediately with one another as neighbors. Beginning with September 11, 2001, there have been too many occasions in recent years where we have come together in community to support our brothers and sisters that may be under attack because of the actions of a few associated with their religion. When we gather, we eat, talk, and listen to one another.

Interfaith cooperation does not necessarily mean worshipping together, which may violate the uniqueness of religious ritual. The book *Getting to the Heart of Interfaith* demonstrates an interfaith association between a pastor, a rabbi and a sheikh. Interfaith work is a journey or a process, wherein participants engage in self-examination as well as learning, coming to respect both the differences and commonalities among their faith traditions.[26] While observing one another in worship, they may not actually engage in common prayer. Yet interfaith understanding always involves the sacred act of listening.

Communities of faith also uphold one another through listening, in times of pain and suffering. Bradley Hanson, my friend and Religion professor in college, was the first person to teach me the value of silence and meditation. He describes in his book *The Call of Silence* a painful time in both his and my life.[27] His family, along with fifteen other college students and I, lived in a house in Nottingham, England my junior year of college. The next fall,

26 Mackenzie, et al., *Getting to the Heart.*

27. Hanson, *Call of Silence*, 56–62. See more on Christian meditation throughout this book as well as in Hanson, *Teach Us to Pray.*

Mike, our good friend and member of our Nottingham family, committed suicide back on the Luther College campus.

Brad recalls how there were many forms of prayer that became important during the days following Mike's death: corporate prayer in worship, silent meditative prayer, and especially the prayers we voiced as we gathered together, made more meaningful because of our bond of friendship. Whatever it was we said, we gathered together in Presence and were present with one another in community. It was there the healing of our grief began.

In many ways it was Mike's death that started me on a spiritual journey of questioning. Until then, I was a member of campus Christian groups and quite satisfied with a Parental God figure and a pretty clear-cut understanding of good and bad, heaven and hell. But Mike's death was the crisis that jolted me into a long journey of seeking to open my eyes. I suddenly questioned doctrines I had held to be unchanging. How could God condemn such a person, I wondered? Mike was not perfect, as none of us were, and was not a believer in a traditional sense. Yet, he was present as a good friend, had an incredibly compassionate heart for the oppressed, he was loving, and above all he was loved. That love overrode any judgment and permeated our life as a community.

Every person and community will find many more ways than these to learn to listen and to strengthen connections together. In doing so, we will compel one another to move deeper into our journey of faith. Our personal lives and our religious lives are filled with countless opportunities to stop judging, to listen, and to love one another in our joy and in our sadness. Prayer and discussions can be approached with a spirit of listening, rather than doctrinal answers and right dogma. We can share in open-ended ways and learn to listen in all of our meetings and encounters, both within and outside the church.

Opening our eyes, at its most radical, is being fully present with one another. We can learn from Jesus and from many traditions. Opening our eyes moves us toward a new way of living as members of a global community. We look to the traditions around us, learning from others who have discovered ways ritual carries individuals within the context of community, into a deep place of Presence. One of our greatest tasks is to celebrate Jesus and the truth he offers, as well as his Presence in our lives, without becoming exclusive, judgmental, unforgiving, and discriminatory in our actions and doctrine. We are called to a new way—to open our eyes, to listen, to watch and to awaken to Presence wherever it is, and to live in the present in community.

Conclusion

Letting Go of Truth

TWO HUGE crises face us today, as we long for peace in our lives. The first is a crisis of soul. We are disconnected from our roots, our religious traditions, even our own selves, and we yearn for depth and meaning in our lives, and for a sense of inner peace. Second, we live in a world where environmental devastation looms, where millions do not have enough to eat, where children are growing up in abusive homes and war-torn lands. These two are not unrelated. Becoming more peaceful and grounded as persons will help us to show compassion to one another, to treat our environment with respect, and to bring about positive change.

Indeed, our world is at a precipice—where we may all fall in together due to problems caused by hunger and overpopulation and environmental damage, exacerbated by wars (often waged in the name of religion) and greed in all its manifestations. As we teeter on this brink, we need to recall one of the greatest lessons we find in many wisdom traditions calling us to let go. We are called upon to live more radically as persons who let go than at any time in the history of humankind. When we drop our own egos and our own insistence on being right, we can begin the process of listening to one another and of healing.

Jesus said the one who "loses the self will gain it." For Christians, that letting go will include everything—not just a dependence upon oil and material superiority, but even the doctrines and dogmas that we insist are glossier and superior to all others. Reconciliation does not have room for egoistic claims—only for love and true respect.

Once we let go of our control and live in Presence, we will face ourselves, we will change, and we will find ourselves compelled to engage in justice and compassion in the world. Letting go overcomes dualistic polemics between human beings, and opens up a new way to understand what Jesus calls us to. It is meant to echo a way—the way that the apostle Mark writes about that Jesus was paving in his ministry on his three-year trip from Galilee to Jerusalem. This is the way of compassion.

We cannot bring back the past, nor can we bring the future to us. All we have is the present. Our search for inner peace centers us in the present, deeply and fully. This grounding does not require us to hold a doctrine that excludes those who believe differently. None of us has a monopoly on truth, or the Divine. Looking at the life of Jesus and fundamentally why he was killed moves us toward truth that is not exclusive or just about ourselves. It is about the entire earth and those who suffer in any way. Jesus offers a message for all of humanity, not just an exclusive group calling themselves Christians. For any who yearn for a world of compassion, we can learn from the reality Jesus called God's world, here on earth. A world where we exclude no one, but welcome all with justice and love.

Some on a serious spiritual journey today have rejected religion, especially Christianity, as holding any real truth. Many are finding rewarding spiritual paths outside religion. Others continue to identify as Christians, attending church and helping their neighbors. Some may question: isn't all this talk about radical presence and inner peace heretical?

No, because as broken human beings we can never really know eternal truths, or know exactly what God intends in this tiny moment in time and for every person on earth throughout all time. If we are to ask difficult questions about our theology, we have to begin with confession. Every time we claim the truth, we have to confess in the same breath that, frankly, we might be wrong. Buddhists have a saying, "If you meet the Buddha on the road, kill him." Similarly, if we think we know the mind of God, it simply cannot be—so we need to kill our idea and start over. Once again, we are confronted with those powerful words: "The first will be last, and the last will be first." If we insist on being the saved, the ones who hold the only truth, the bearers of salvation itself, we are negating the very message of humility and love offered in Jesus' gospel.

Learning to live in Presence along our spiritual search is vital for those of us who may or may not practice a particular religion, but who also get extremely lonely, who feel pain deeply, who experience suffering, and who in spite of trying to do everything right, never quite feel fulfilled. It is for those who long for an end to the weariness of a world at war. It is for those who long for peace within.

It is time to take seriously a new kind of reign on earth that was introduced by Jesus and has been proposed by founders and prophets of many religions, but has been ignored. Jesus invites those who have ears to hear to listen. Come away to a lonely place, and make your prayer an act of listening. Jesus beckons those who have eyes to see, to watch, sit, learn and finally act, developing compassion for yourself, your community, and your world. Jesus asks whether anyone is willing to stay awake with him. Awaken to Presence within and around you.

Give yourself the gift of letting go. Pause, listen, watch, and awaken, ushering in the way of compassion and love.

Bibliography

Achtemeier, Paul J. *Invitation to Mark: A Commentary on the Gospel of Mark.* Garden City, NY: Image Books, 1978.

Allen, Paula Gunn. *Grandmothers of the Light: A Medicine Woman's Sourcebook.* Boston: Beacon, 1991.

Al-Suhrawardy, Allama Abdullah. *The Wisdom of Muhammad.* New York: Citadel, 2001.

Anderson, Janice Capel, and Stephen P. Moore. *Mark & Method.* Minneapolis: Fortresss, 2008.

Anzaldúa, Gloria. *Borderlands: La Frontera.* San Francisco: Aunt Lute Books, 1987.

Arnold, Edwin, trans. *Bhagavadgita.* New York: Dover, 1993.

Armstrong, Karen. *Islam.* New York: The Modern Library, 2002.

Asad, Muhammad, trans. *The Message of the Qur'an.* Bristol, England: The Book Foundation, 2003.

Augustine. *The Confessions of St. Augustine.* Translated by John K. Ryan. Garden City, NY: Image Books, 1960.

Barks, Coleman, with John Moyne. *The Essential Rumi.* San Francisco: HarperSanFrancisco, 1995.

Benhabib, Seyla. *Situating the Self: Gender, Community and Postmodernism in Contemporary Ethics.* New York: Routledge, 1992.

Borg, Marcus J. *Conversations with Scripture: The Gospel of Mark.* Harrisburg, PA: Morehouse, 2009.

———. *Jesus: Uncovering the Life, Teachings, and Relevance of a Religious Revolutionary.* New York: HarperOne, 2006.

Borg, Marcus J, and John Dominic Crossan. *The Last Week: A Day-by-Day Account of Jesus's Final Week in Jerusalem.* San Francisco: HarperSanFrancisco, 2006.

Brach, Tara. *Radical Acceptance: Embracing your Life with the Heart of a Buddha.* New York: Bantam Books, 2003.

Brock, Rita Nakashima, and Rebecca Ann Parker. *Proverbs of Ashes: Violence, Redemptive Suffering, and the Search for What Saves Us.* Boston: Beacon, 2001.

———. *Saving Paradise: How Christianity Traded Love of This World for Crucifixion and Empire.* Boston: Beacon, 2008.

Bibliography

Cardenál, Ernesto. *The Gospel in Solentiname*. Translated by Donald D. Walsh. Vol. 2. Maryknoll, NY: Orbis Books, 1978.

Chittister, Joan D. *Scarred by Struggle, Transformed by Hope*. Grand Rapids, MI: Eerdmans, 2003.

Chödrön, Pema. *Comfortable with Uncertainty: 108 Teachings*. Edited by Emily Hilburn Sell. Boston: Shambhala, 2002.

———. *The Places That Scare You: A Guide to Fearlessness in Difficult Times*. Boston: Shambhala, 2001.

Cleary, Thomas, trans. *The Essential Tao*. San Francisco: HarperSanFrancisco, 1991.

Clément, Olivier. *Taizé: A Meaning to Life*. Chicago: GIA, 1997.

Collins, Adela Yarbro. *Mark*. Edited by Harold W. Attridge. Minneapolis: Fortress, 2007.

Cone, James H. *Risks of Faith: The Emergence of a Black Theology of Liberation, 1968–1998*. Boston: Beacon, 1999.

Cousineau, Phil. *The Art of Pilgramage: The Seeker's Guide to Making Travel Sacred*. York Beach, ME: Conari, 1998.

Crossan, John Dominic. *Jesus: A Revolutionary Biography*. San Francisco: HarperSanFrancisco, 1994.

———. *The Birth of Christianity: Discovering What Happened in the Years Immediately After the Execution of Jesus*. San Francisco: HarperSanFrancisco, 1998.

———. *The Historical Jesus: The Life of a Mediterranean Jewish Peasant*. San Francisco: HarperSanFrancisco, 1991.

Crossan, John Dominic, and Jonathan L. Reed. *Excavating Jesus: Beneath the Stones, Behind the Texts*. San Francisco: HarperSanFrancisco, 2001.

The Dalai Lama, with Howard C. Cutler. *The Art of Happiness: A Handbook for Living*. New York: Riverhead Books, 1998.

The Dalai Lama. *How to Practice: The Way to a Meaningful Life*. Translated by Jeffrey Hopkins. New York: Atria Books, 2002.

Daly, Mary. *Beyond God the Father: Toward a Philosophy of Women's Liberation*. Boston: Beacon, 1973.

Edinger, Edward F. *Ego and Archetype: Individuation and the Religious Function of the Psyche*. Middlesex, England: Penguin Books, 1973, 1980.

Fortune, Marie. *Love Does No Harm: Sexual Ethics for the Rest of Us*. New York: Continuum, 1995.

Fowler, Jim, and Sam Keen. *Life Maps: Conversations on the Jouney of Faith*. Edited by Jerome Berryman. Waco, TX: Word Books, 1978.

Fox, Matthew. *Original Blessing*. New York: Jeremy P. Tarcher/Putnam, 1983.

Gilligan, Carol. *In a Different Voice*. Cambridge: Harvard University Press, 1982.

Goodall, Jane, with Phillip Berman. *Reason for Hope: A Spiritual Journey.* New York: Warner Books, 1999.

Grant, Jacquelyn. "The Sin of Servanthood and the Deliverance of Discipleship." In *A Troubling in My Soul: Womanist Perspectives on Evil alnd Suffering,* edited by Emilie M. Townes, 199–218. Maryknoll, NY: Orbis Books, 1993.

Gutiérrez, Gustavo. *We Drink from Our Own Wells: The Spiritual Journey of a People.* Maryknoll, NY: Orbis Books, 2003.

Hanson, Bradley. *Teach Us to Pray: Overcoming Obstacles to Daily Prayer.* Minneapolis: Augsburg Fortress, 1990.

———. *The Call of Silence: Discovering Christian Meditation.* Minneapolis: Augsburg, 1980.

Harjo, Joy. *How We Became Human: New and Selected Poems: 1975–2001.* New York: W.W. Norton & Company, 2002.

Helminski, Kabir Edmund. *Living Presence: A Sufi Way to Mindfulness and the Essential Self.* New York: Jeremy P. Tarcher/Putnam, 1992.

Heschel, Abraham Joshua. *The Sabbath.* New York: Farrar, Straus and Giroux, 1951.

Heyward, Carter. *Saving Jesus From Those Who Are Right.* Minneapolis: Augsburg Fortress, 1999.

The Holy Bible, Revised Standard Version. New York, Oxford University Press, 1962, 1973.

The Jane Austen Book Club. Directed by Robin Swicord. Sony Pictures Classics, 2007.

John of the Cross. *Dark Night of the Soul.* Translated by Mirabai Starr. New York: Riverhead Books, 2002.

Jung, C. G. *Memories, Dreams, Reflections.* Edited by Aniela Jaffé. Translated by Richard & Clara Winston. New York: Vintage Books, 1965.

Katie, Byron, with Stephen Mitchell. *Loving What Is: Four Questions That Can Change Your Life.* New York: Three Rivers, 2002.

Keating, Thomas. *The Mystery of Christ: The Liturgy as Christian Experience.* Rockport, MA: Element, 1991.

———. *Open Mind, Open Heart: The Contemplative Dimension of the Gospel.* New York: Continuum, 1996.

Kirby, Vicki. *Judith Butler: Live Theory.* New York: Continuum, 2006.

Lindvall, Michael A. *A Geography of God: Exploring the Christian Journey.* Louisville: Westminster John Knox, 2007.

Mackenzie, Don, et al. *Getting to the Heart of Interfaith: The Eye-Opening Friendship of a Pastor, a Rabbi and a Sheikh.* Woodstock, VT: Skylight Paths, 2009.

Bibliography

Maguire, Jack. *Essential Buddhism: A Complete Guide to Beliefs and Practices.* New York: Pocket Books, 2001.

Marty, Martin. *When Faiths Collide.* Malden, MA: Blackwell, 2005.

McFague, Sallie. *The Body of God: An Ecological Theology.* Minneapolis: Fortress, 1993.

McLennan, Scotty. *Finding Your Religion: When the Faith You Grew Up With Has Lost Its Meaning.* San Francisco: HarperSanFrancisco, 1999.

Merton, Thomas. *The Inner Experience: Notes on Contemplation.* Edited by William H. Shannon. San Francisco: HarperSanFrancisco, 2003.

Meyer, Marvin W., trans. *The Secret Teachings of Jesus: Four Gnostic Gospels.* New York: Vintage Books, 1986.

Moore, Thomas. *Care of the Soul: A Guide for Cultivating Depth and Sacredness in Everyday Life.* New York: HarperPerennial, 1992.

Myers, Ched. *Binding the Strong Man: A Political Reading of Mark's Story of Jesus.* Maryknoll, NY: Orbis Books, 1988, 2008.

Nhat Hanh, Thich. *Living Buddha, Living Christ.* New York: Riverhead Books, 1995.

The New Jerusalem Bible. Garden City, NY: Doubleday, 1985.

Olsen, Tillie. *Silences.* New York: Delta/Seymour Lawrence, 1965, 1978.

Pagels, Elaine. *Beyond Belief: The Secret Gospel of Thomas.* New York: Random House, 2003.

———. *The Gnostic Gospels.* New York: Vintage Books, 1979.

Palmer, E. H., trans. *The Koran.* London: Watkins, 2007.

Palmer, Parker. *Let Your Life Speak: Listening For the Voice of Vocation.* San Francisco: Jossey-Bass, 2000.

The Passion of the Christ. Directed by Mel Gibson. Icon Distribution Films, Inc., 2003.

Pennington, M. Basil. *Centering Prayer: Renewing an Ancient Christian Form of Prayer.* New York: Image Books, 1982.

Perrin, Norman. *The Resurrection According to Matthew, Mark, and Luke.* Philadelphia: Fortress, 1977.

Radecke, Mark Wm. "Misguided Missions." *The Christian Century* 127, no. 10 (May 2010) 22–25.

Rasmussen, Larry L. *Earth Community Earth Ethics.* Maryknoll, NY: Orbis Books, 1996, 1998.

Rhoads, David, et al. *Mark as Story: An Introduction to the Narrative of a Gospel.* 2d. ed. Minneapolis: Augsburg Fortress, 1999.

Roger of Taizé. *God is Love Alone.* New York: Continuum, 2004.

Ruether, Rosemary Radford. *Gaia & God: An Ecofeminist Theology of Earth Healing.* San Francisco: HarperSanFrancisco, 1992.

Safi, Omid, ed. *Progressive Muslims: On Justice, Gender, and Pluralism.* Oxford, England: OneWorld, 2003.

Saiving, Valerie. "The Human Situation: A Feminine View." In *Womanspirit Rising: A Feminist Reader in Religion,* edited by Carol P. Christ and Judith Plaskow, 25–42. San Francisco: Harper & Row, 1979.

Schneider, David. *Street Zen: The Life and Work of Issan Dorsey.* Boston: Shambhala, 1993.

Smith, Huston. *The Illustrated World's Religions: A Guide to our Wisdom Traditions.* San Francisco: HarperSanFrancisco, 1991, 1994.

Smith, Paul Ely. *Mosaic.* Palouse, WA: Palouse River Music, 2008. Online: http://www.palouserivermusic.com.

St. Clair, Raquel A. *Call and Consequences: A Womanist Reading of Mark.* Minneapolis: Fortress, 2008.

Starhawk. *Dreaming the Dark: Magic, Sex & Politics.* Boston: Beacon, 1982.

Stearns, Gail J. *Writing Pauline: Wisdom from a Long Life.* Lanham, MD: Hamilton Books, 2005.

Teresa of Avila. *The Interior Castle.* Translated by Mirabai Starr. New York: Riverhead Books, 2003.

Tolle, Eckhart. *A New Earth: Awakening to Your Life's Purpose.* New York: Plume Books, 2005.

Townes, Emilie. *Breaking the Fine Rain of Death: African American Health Issues and a Womanist Ethic of Care.* New York: Continuum, 1998.

Trible, Phyllis. *God and the Rhetoric of Sexuality.* Philadelphia: Fortress Press, 1978.

Vogt, Andrea. *Common Courage: Bill Wassmuth, Human Rights and Small Town Activism.* Moscow, ID: University of Idaho Press, 2003.

Williams, Delores S. *Sisters in the Wilderness: The Challenge of Womanist God-Talk.* Maryknoll, NY: Orbis Books, 1993.

Williamson, Jr., Lamar. *Mark.* Atlanta: John Knox, 1983.

Wills, Garry. *What Jesus Meant.* New York: Viking, 2006.

Wolkstein, Diane, and Samuel Noah Kramer. *Inanna: Queen of Heaven and Earth.* New York: Harper & Row, 1983.

Yee, James, with Aimee Molloy. *For God and Country: Faith and Patriotism Under Fire.* New York: PublicAffairs, 2005.